This Book Belongs To The Beautiful :

_____

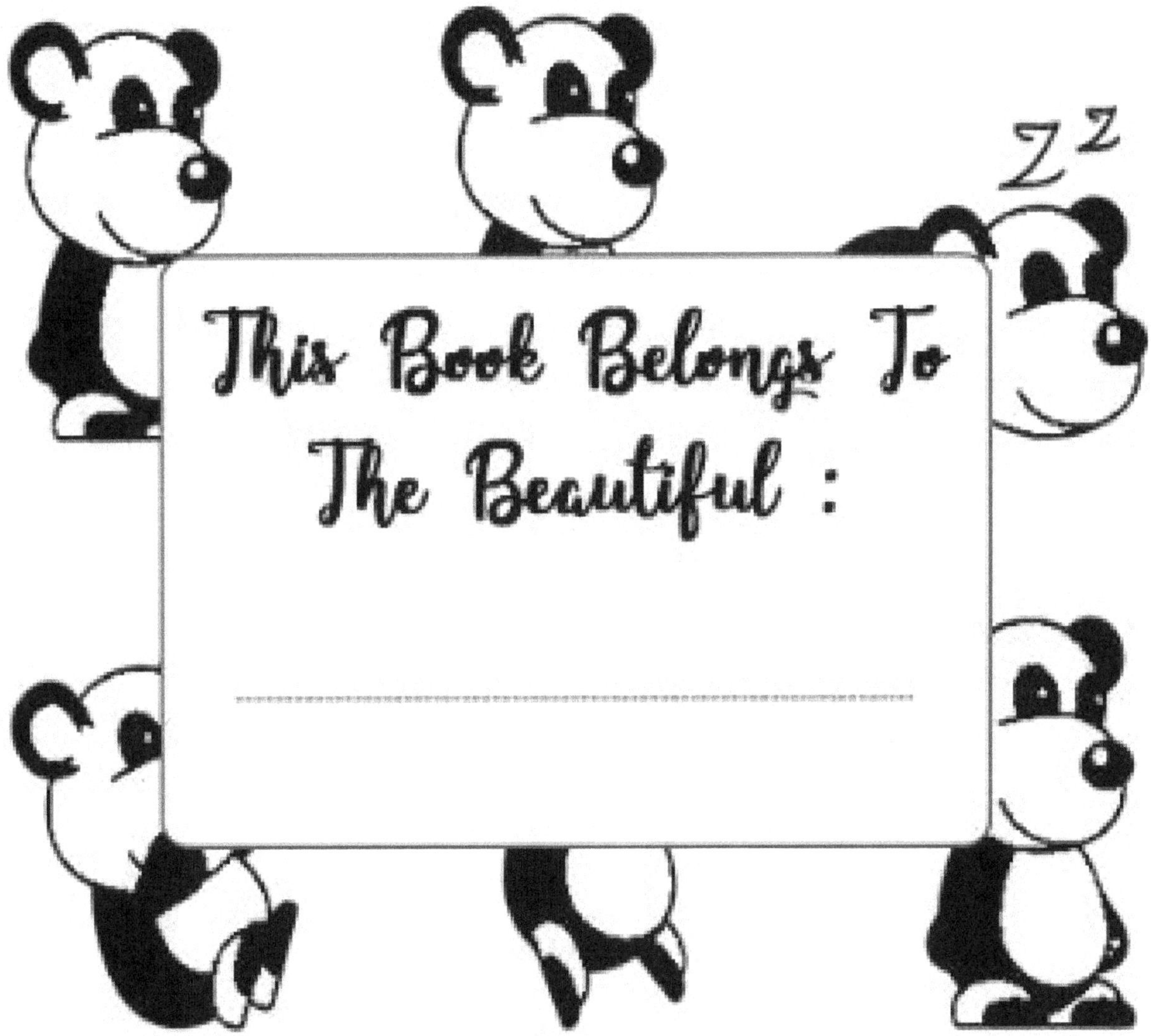

CHEMICAL SCIENTIST

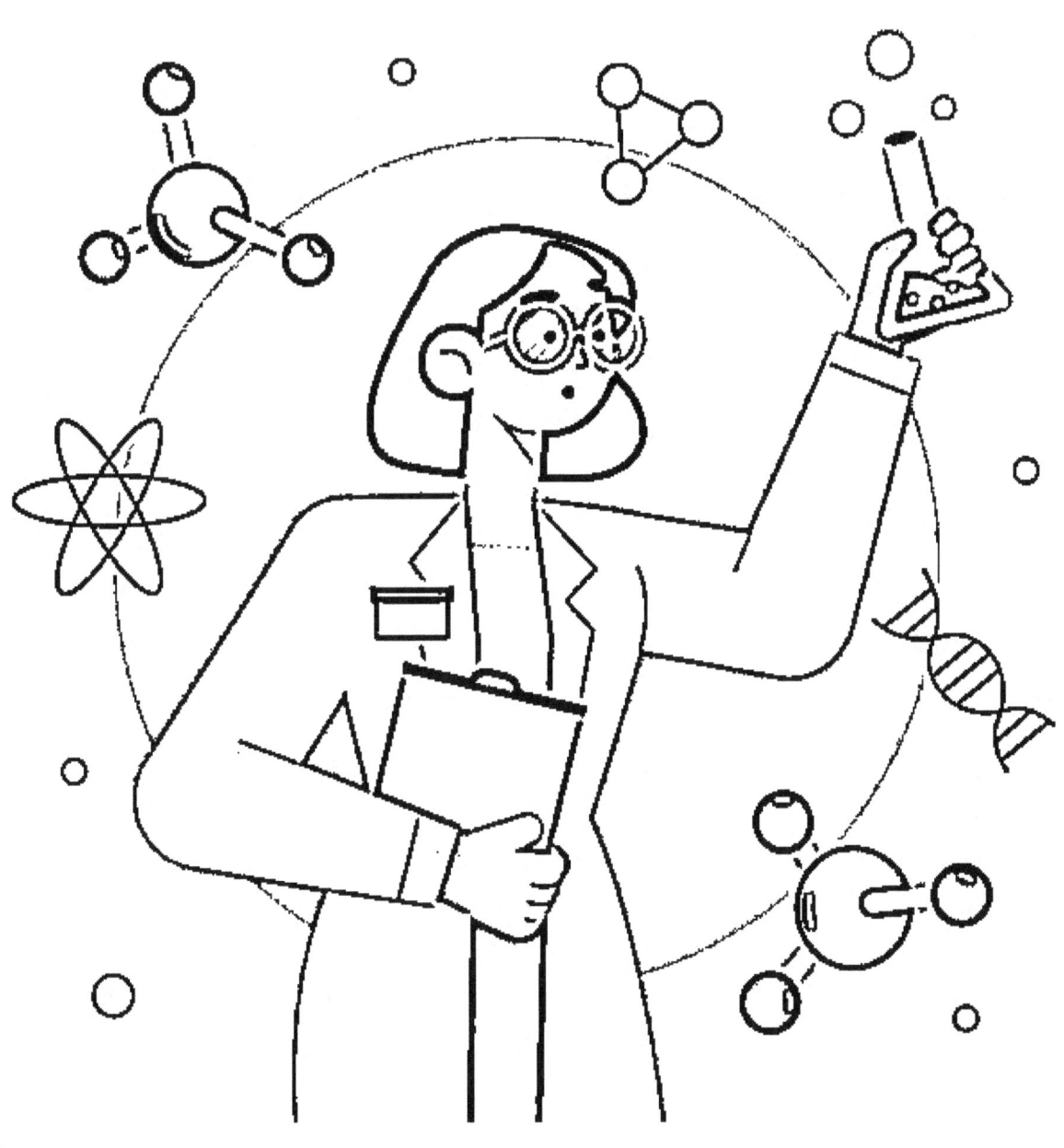

VETERINARIAN

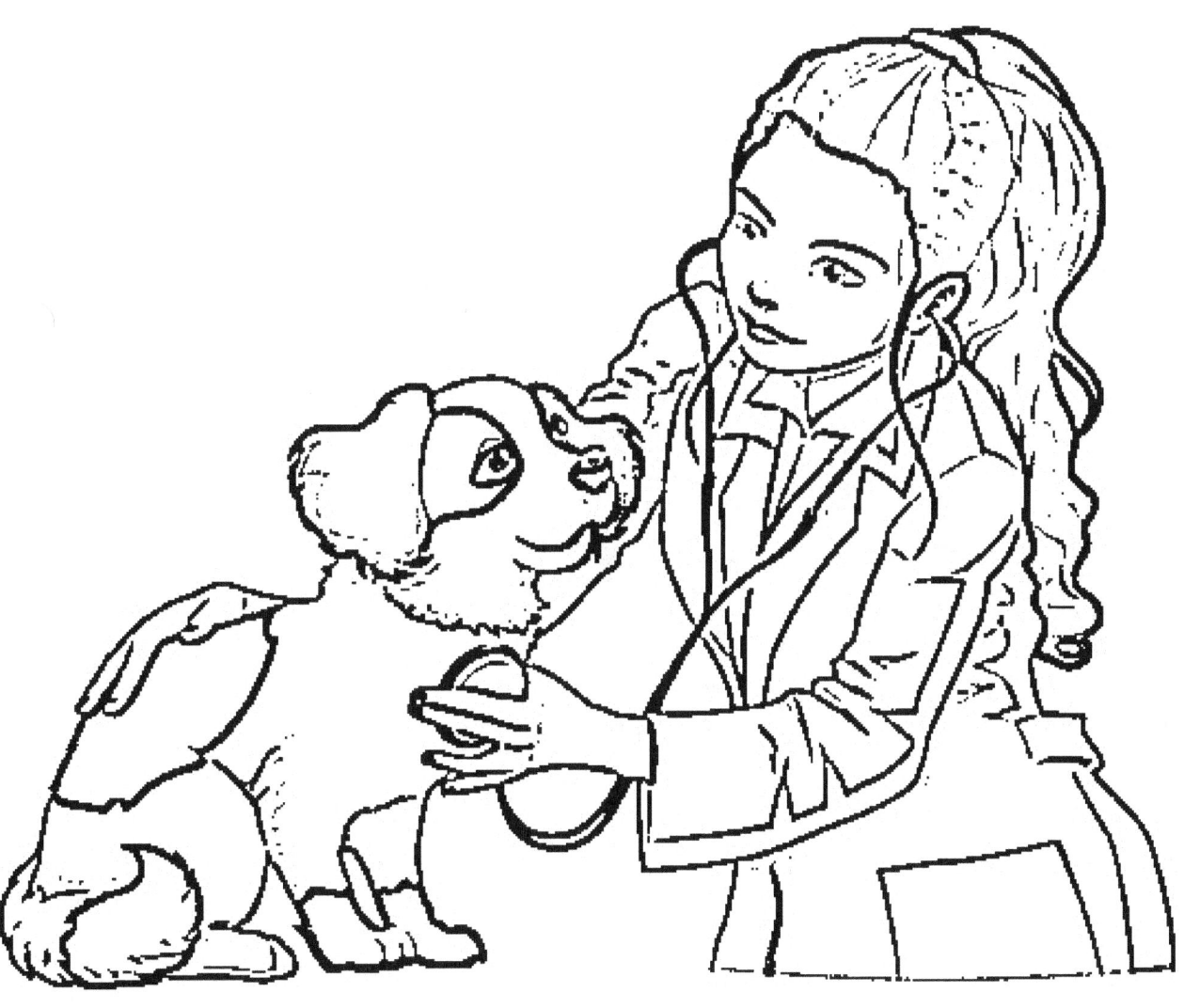

DOCTOR

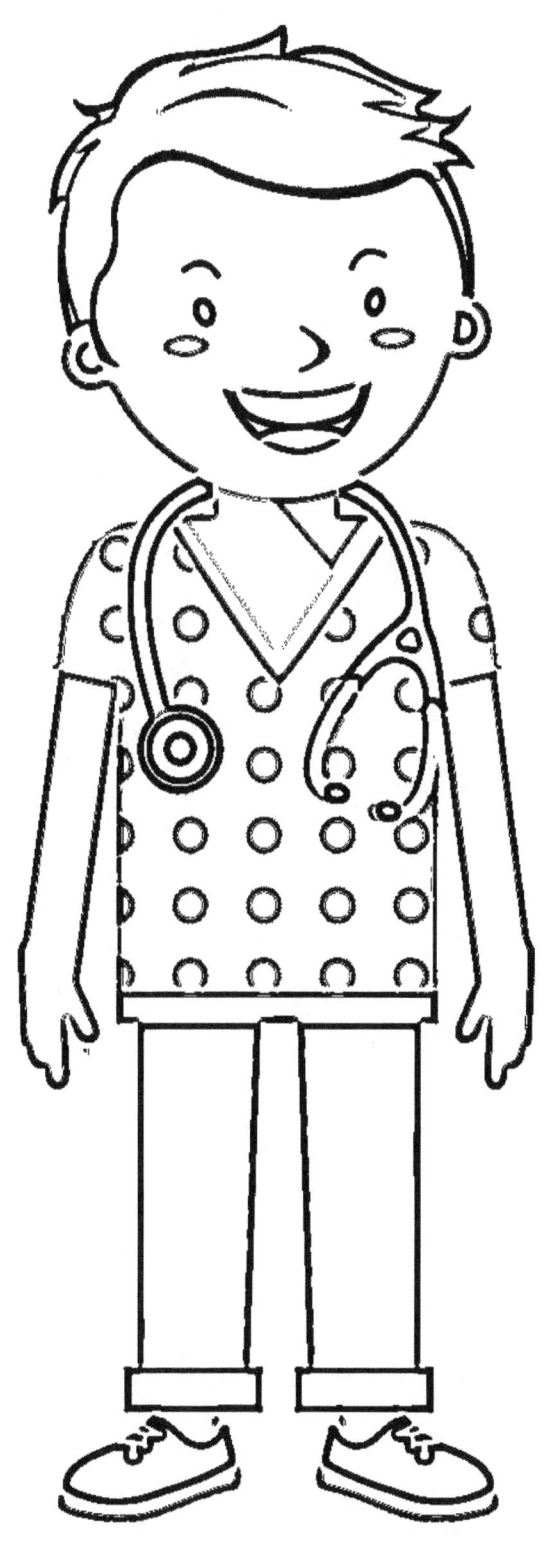

DOCTOR

DENTIST

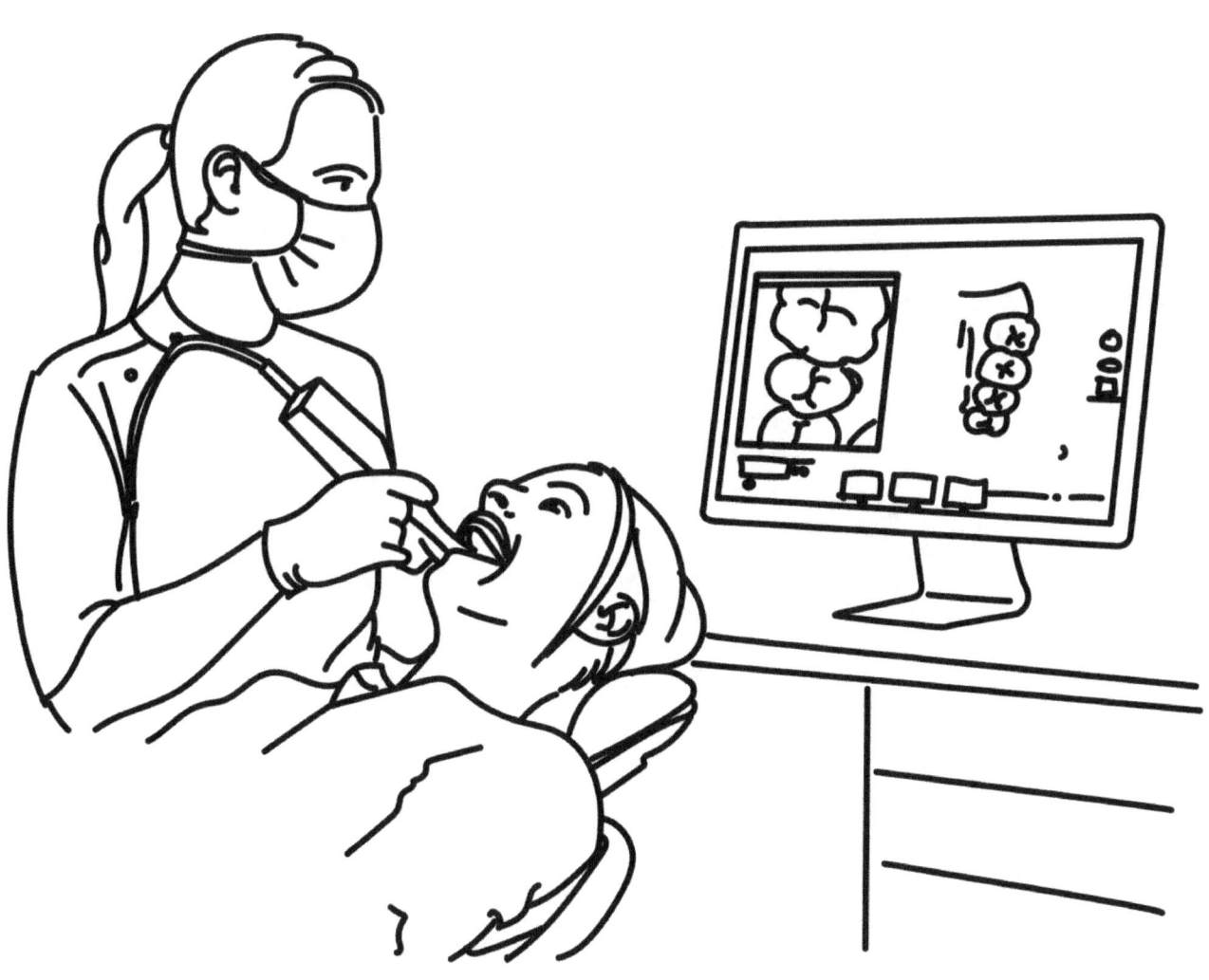

OPHTHALMOLOGIST

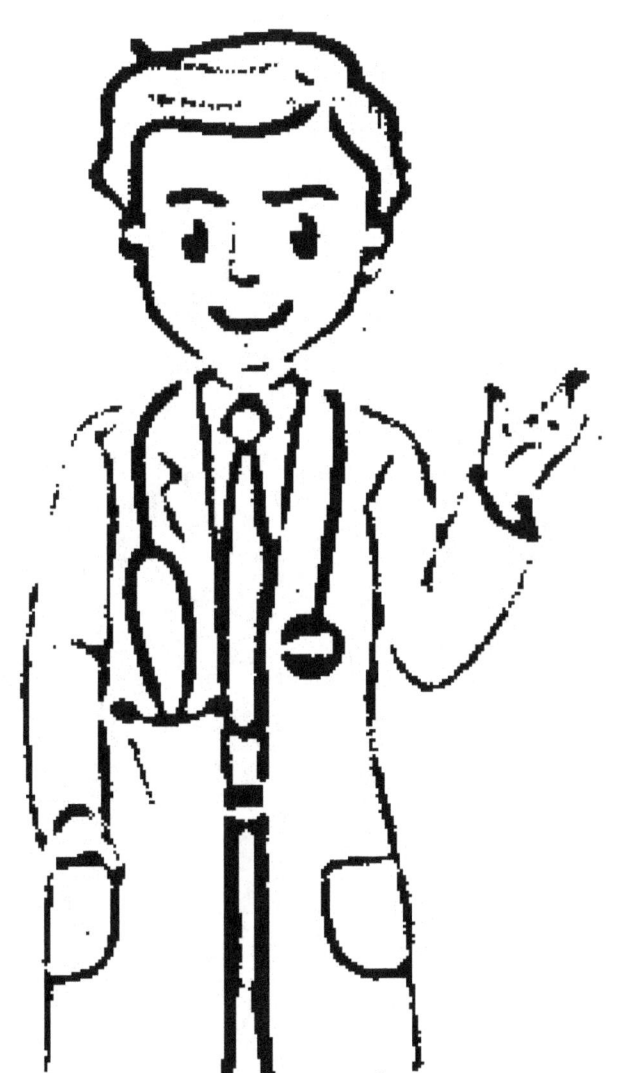

ARCHITECT

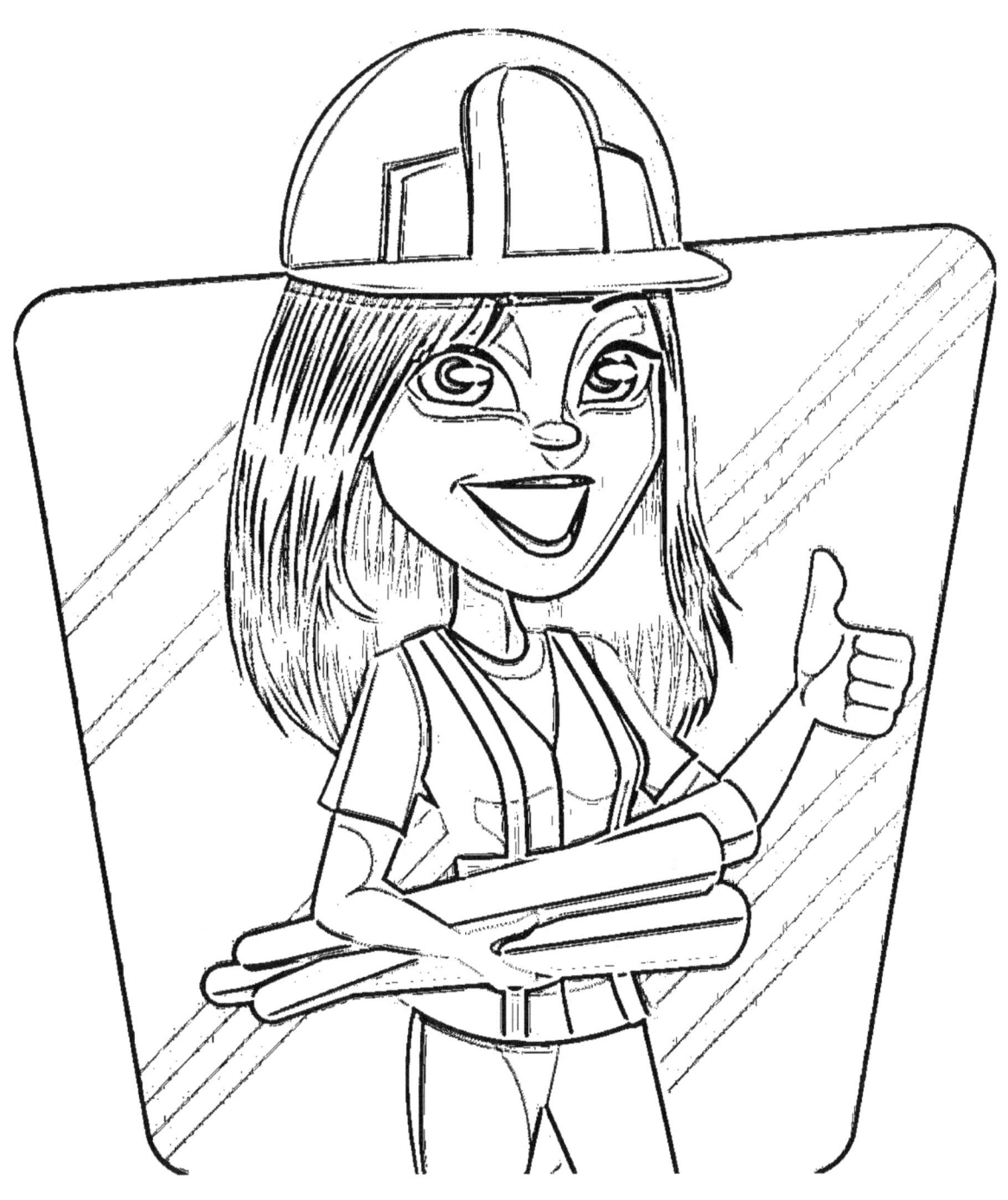

PILOT

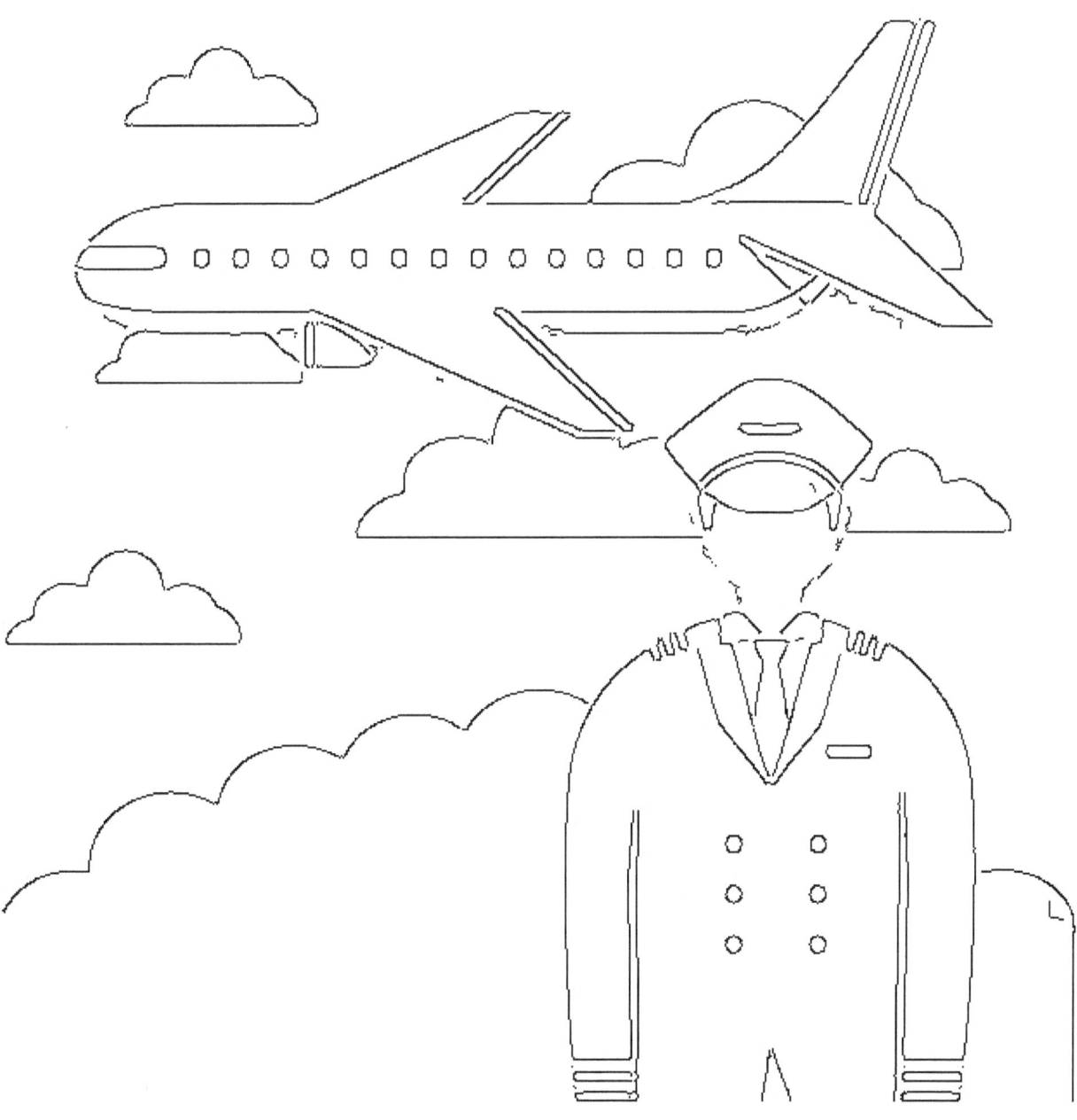

ASTRONAUT

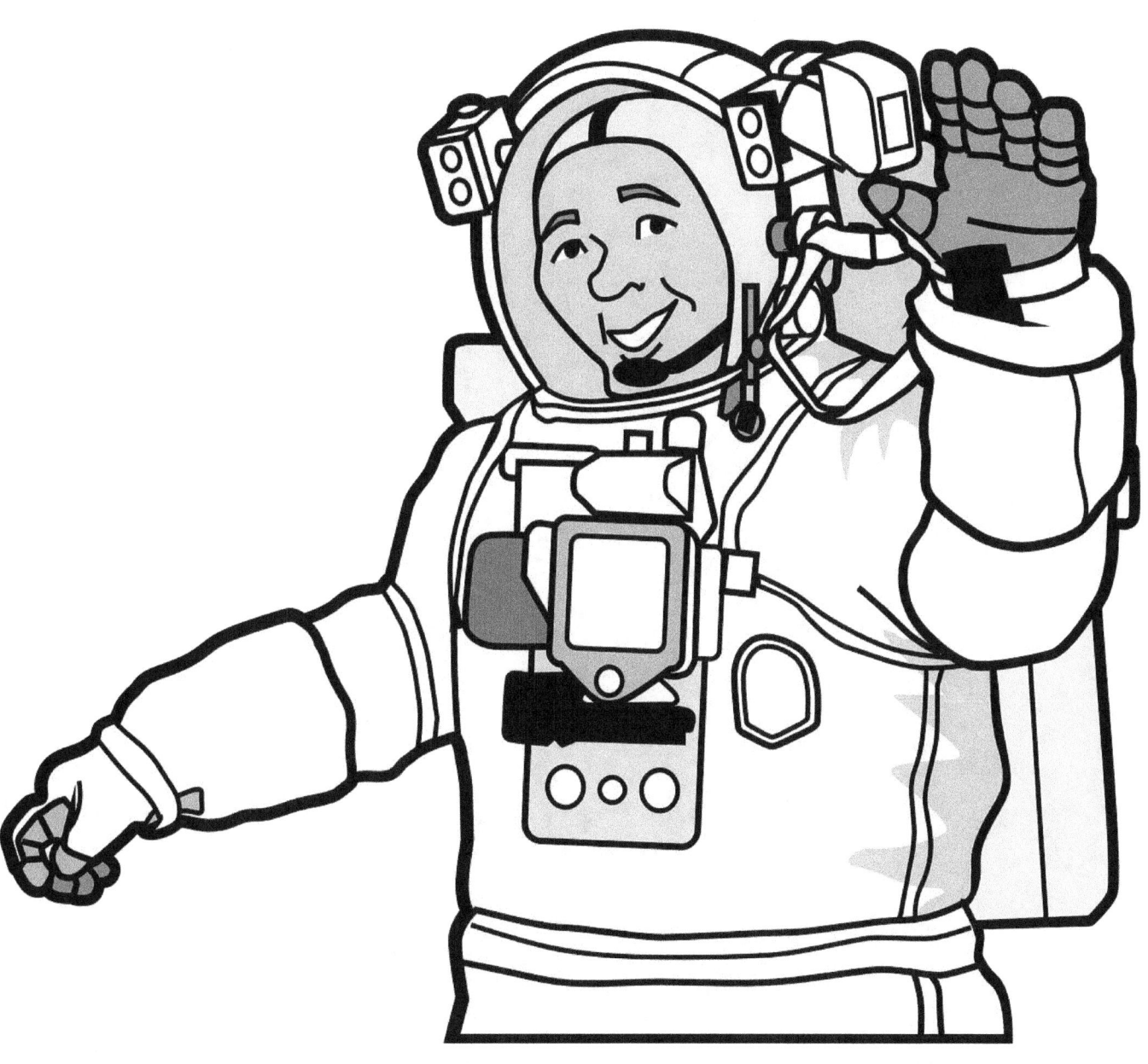

POLICE OFFICER

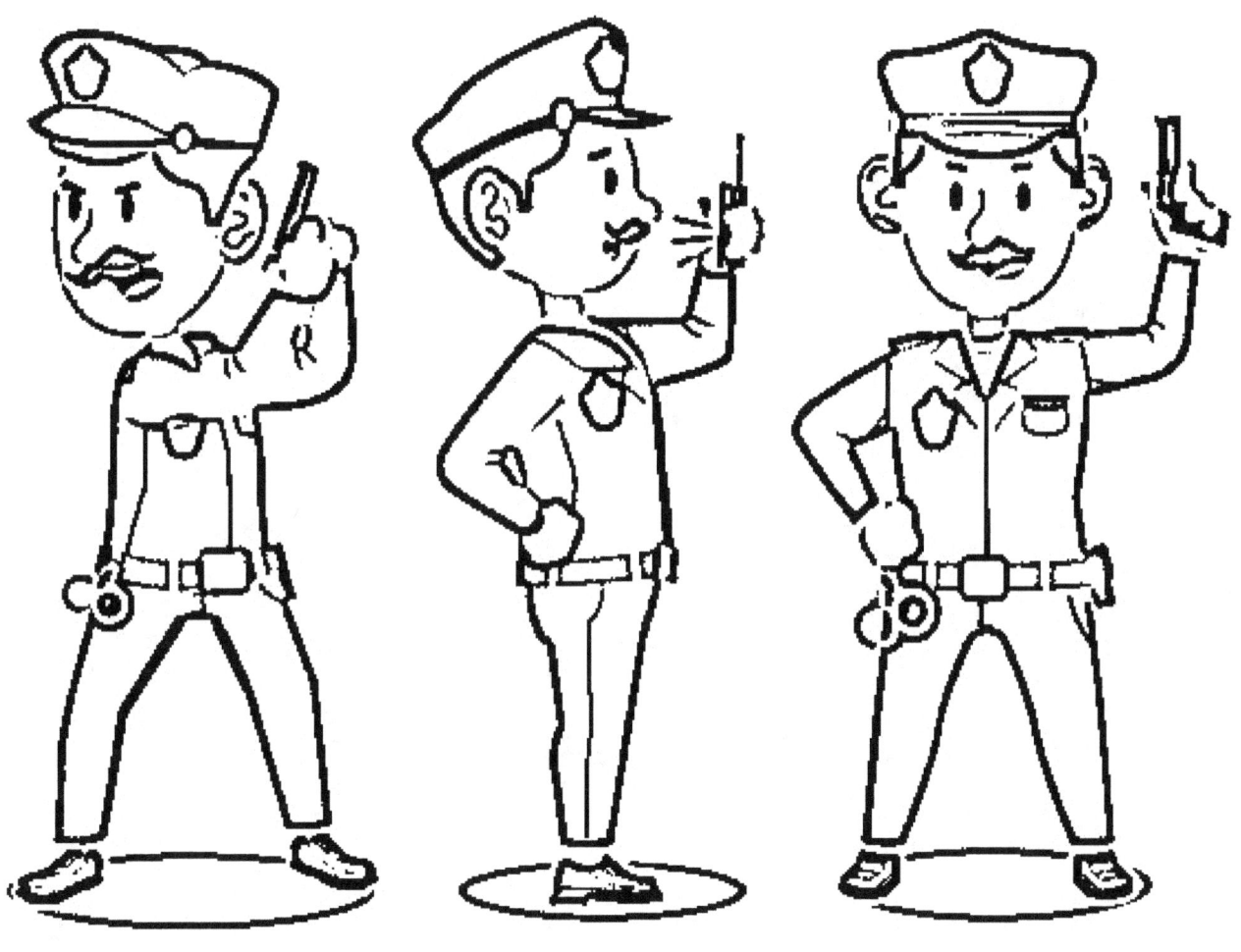

FIREFIGHTER

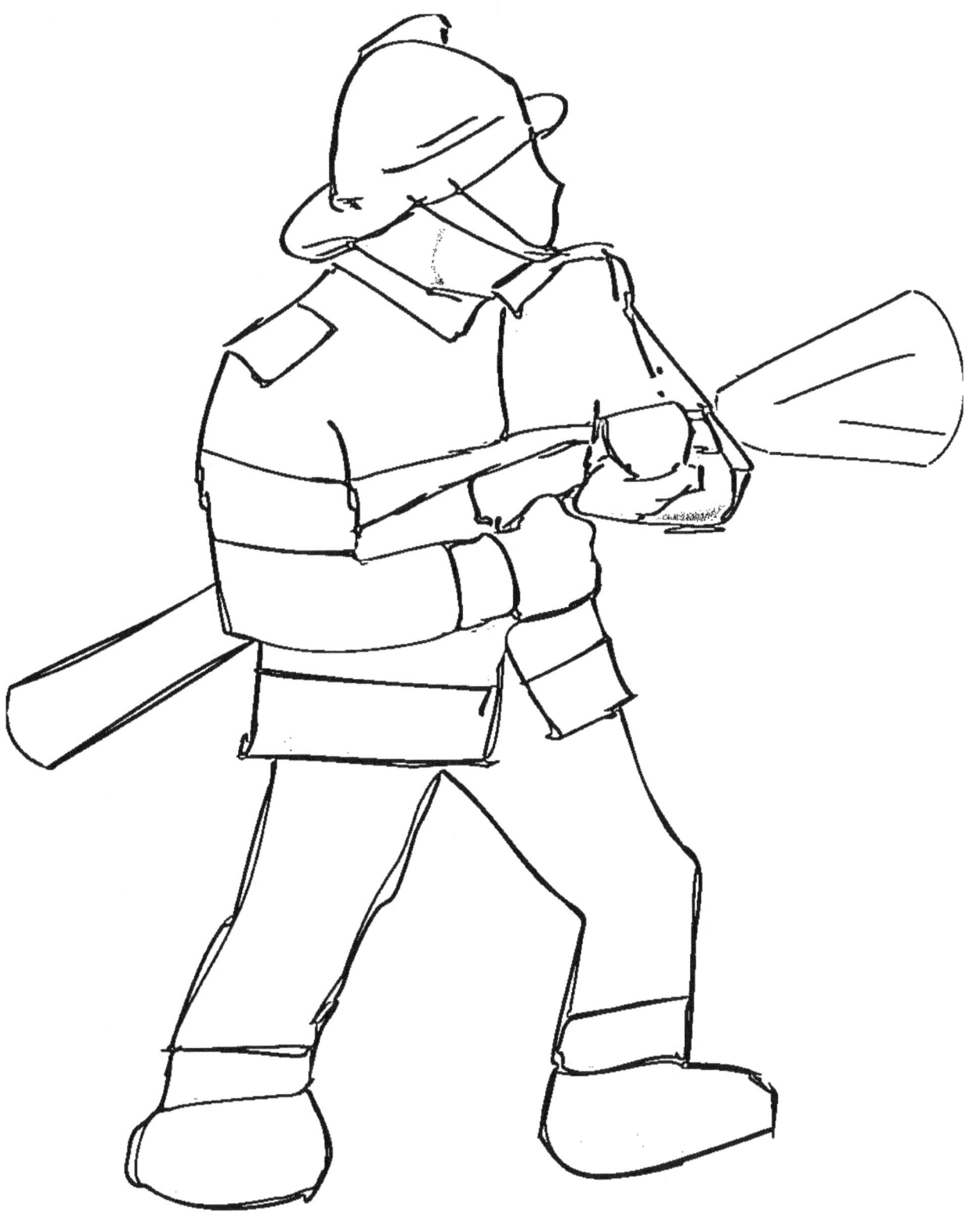

TEACHER

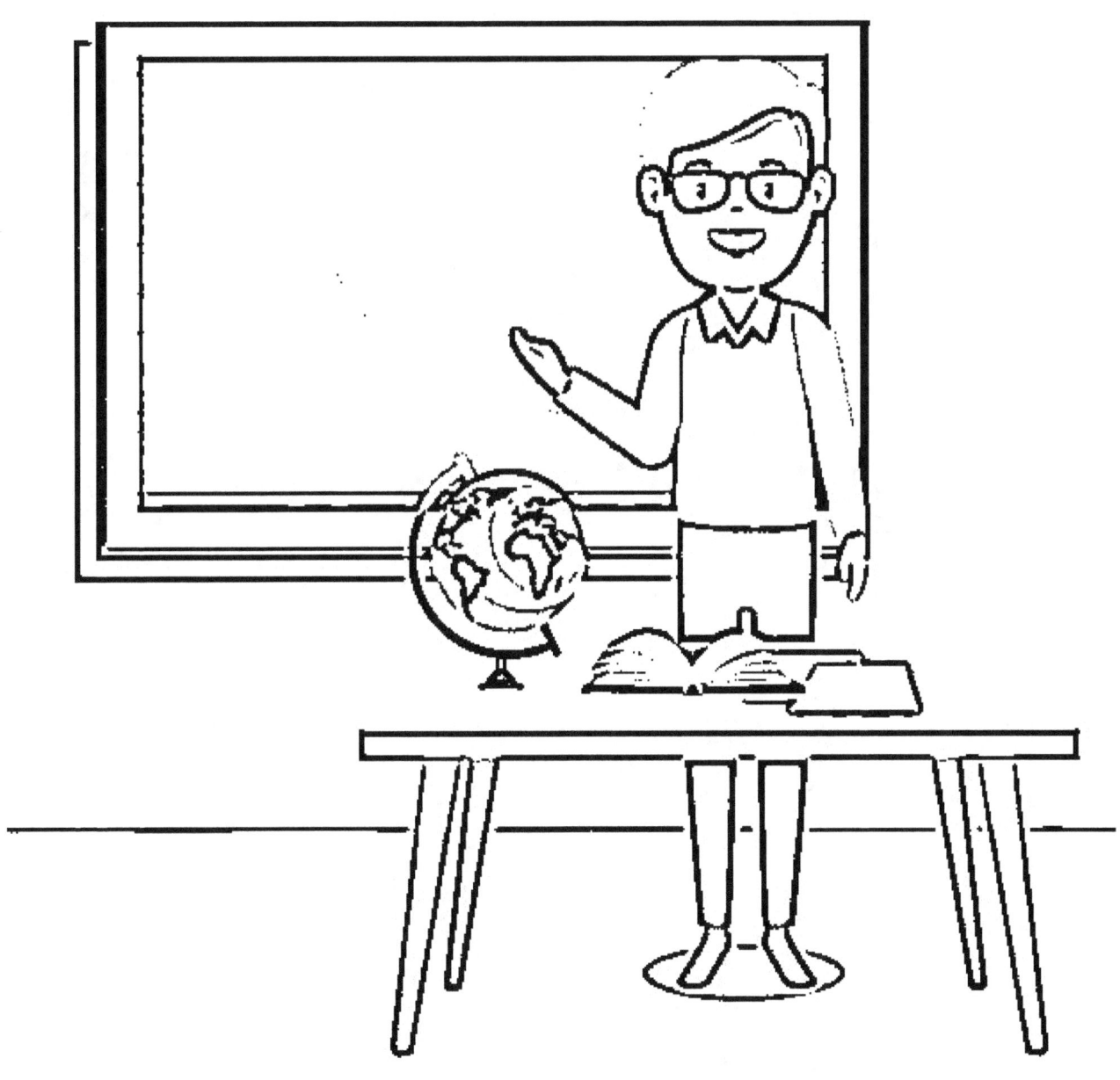

MUSICIAN

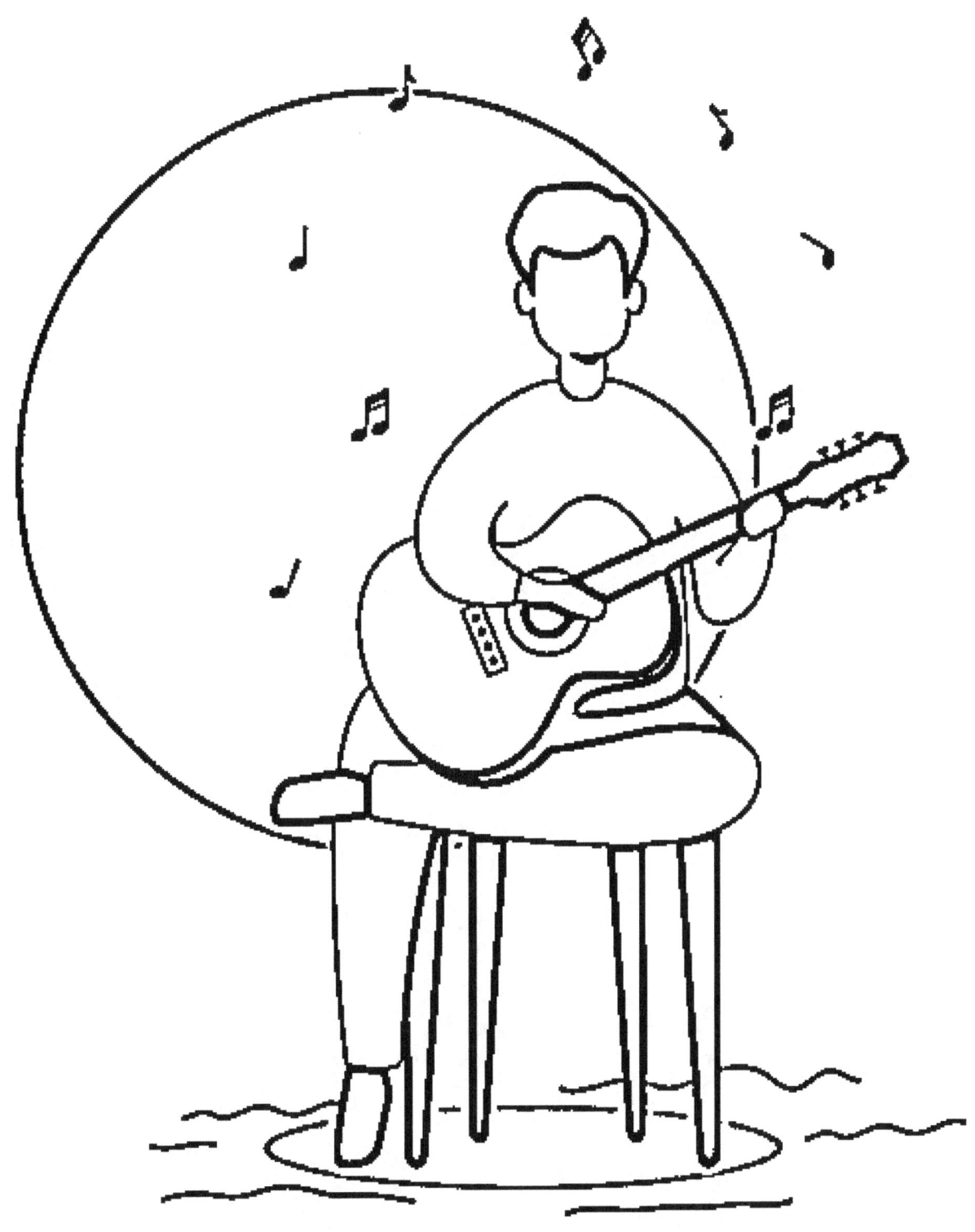

MAGICIAN

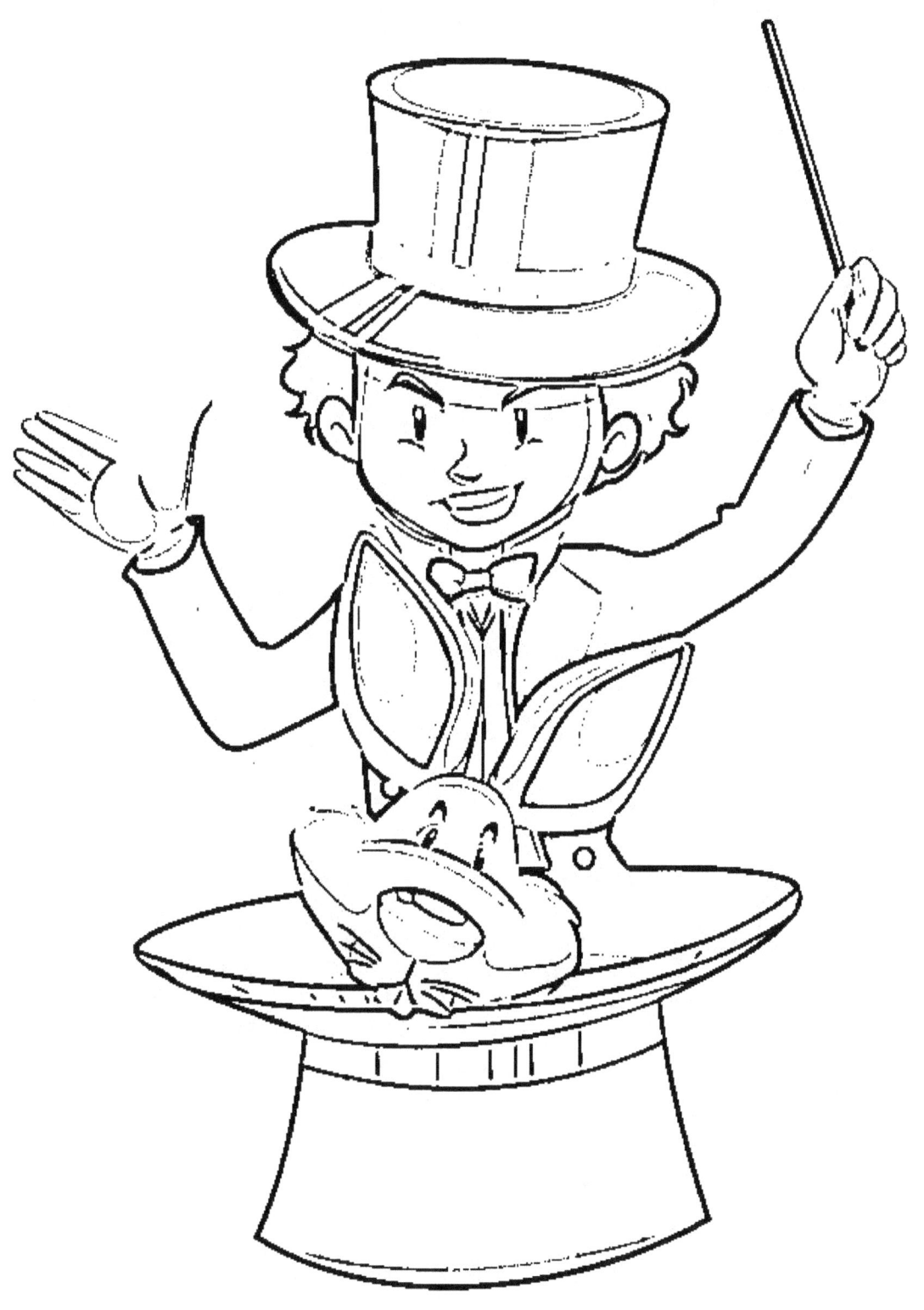

DANCER

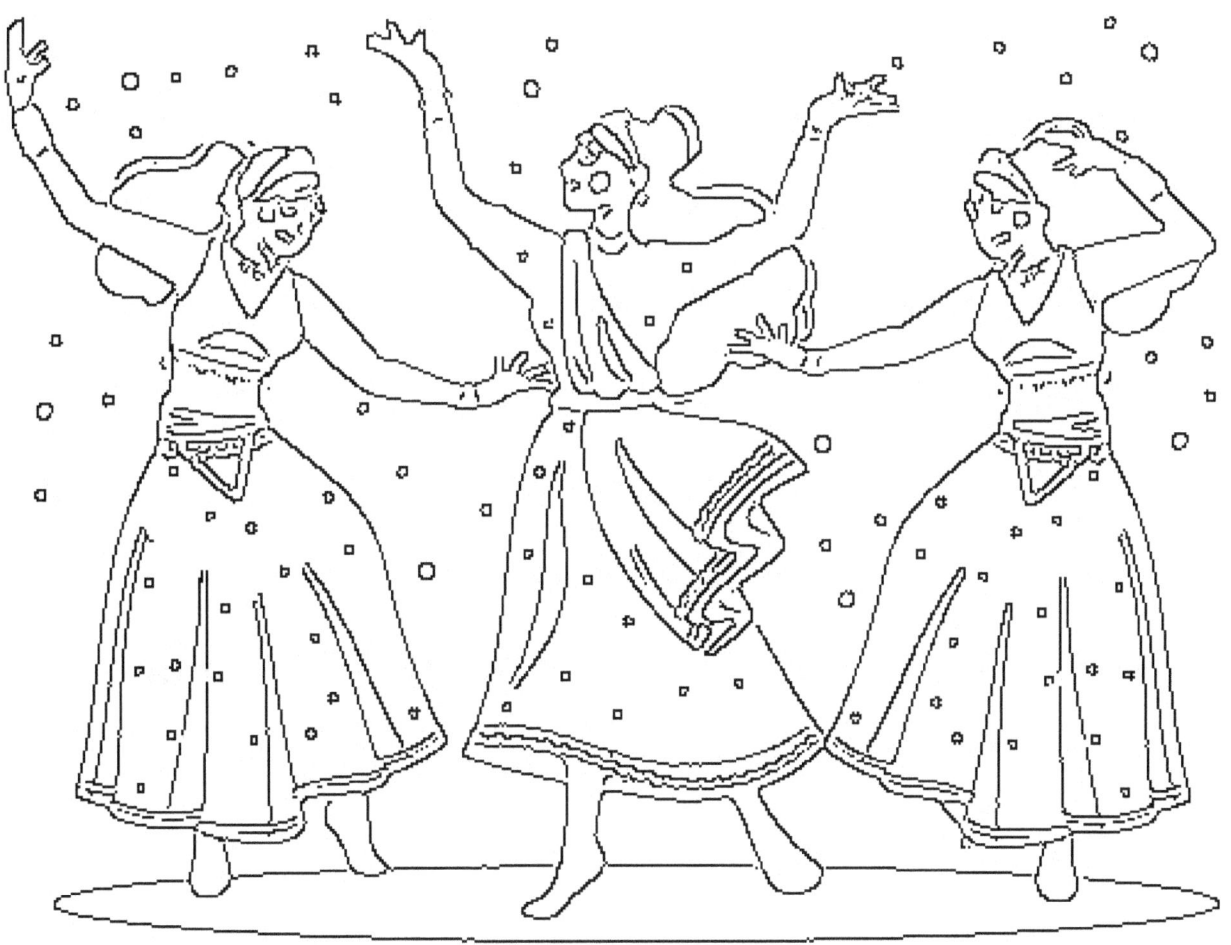

CHEF

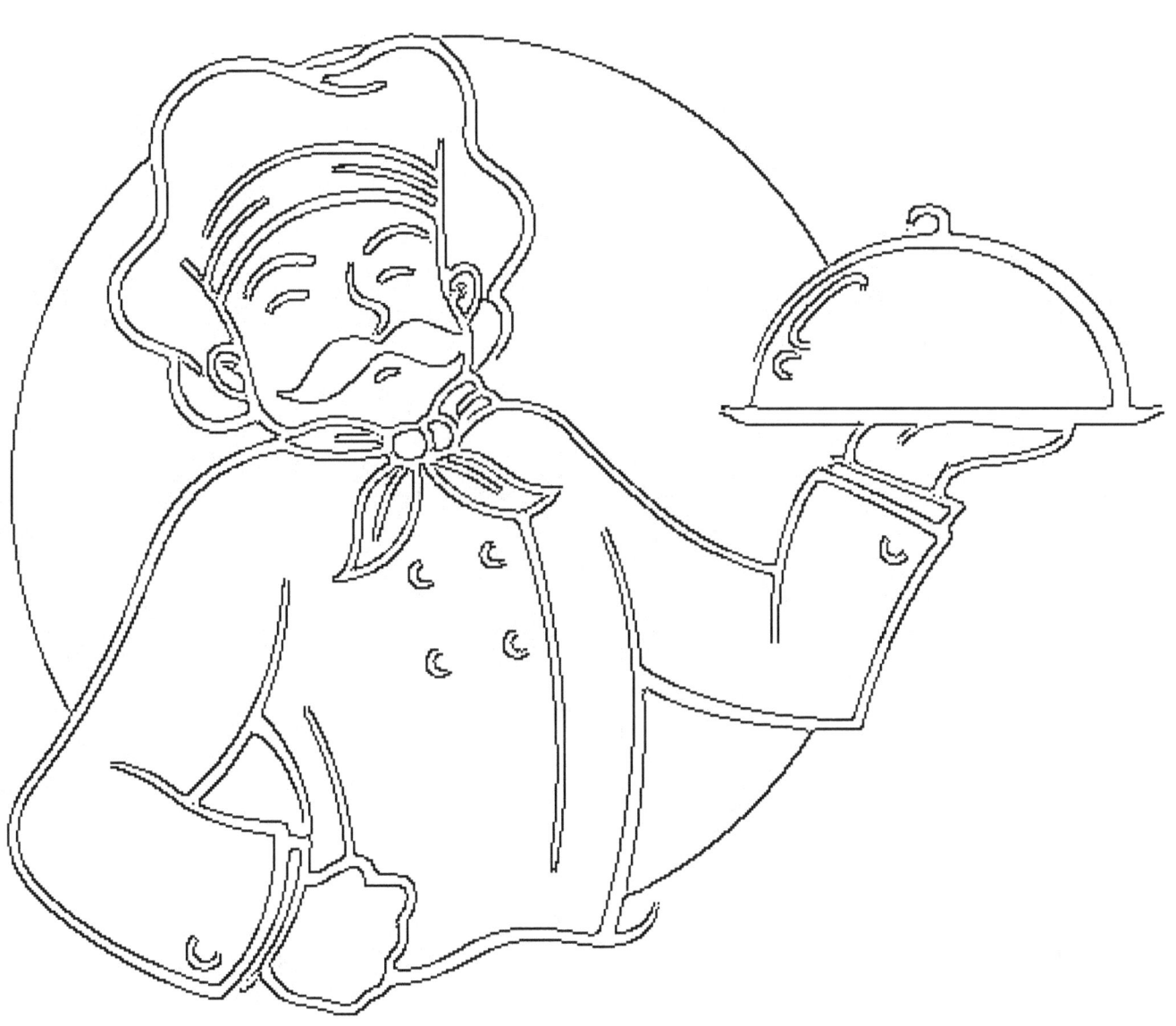

DESIGNER

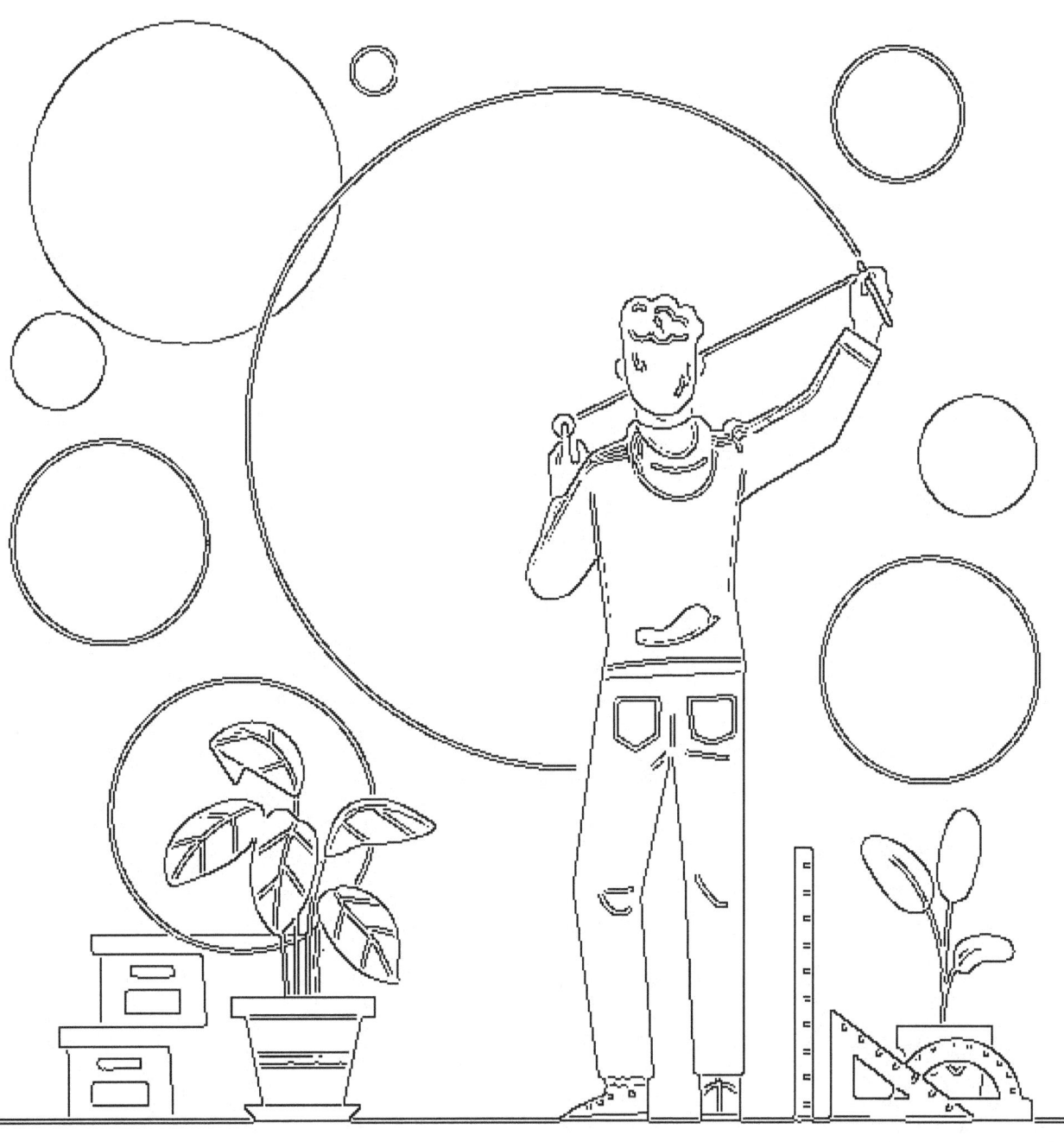

PHOTOGRAPHER

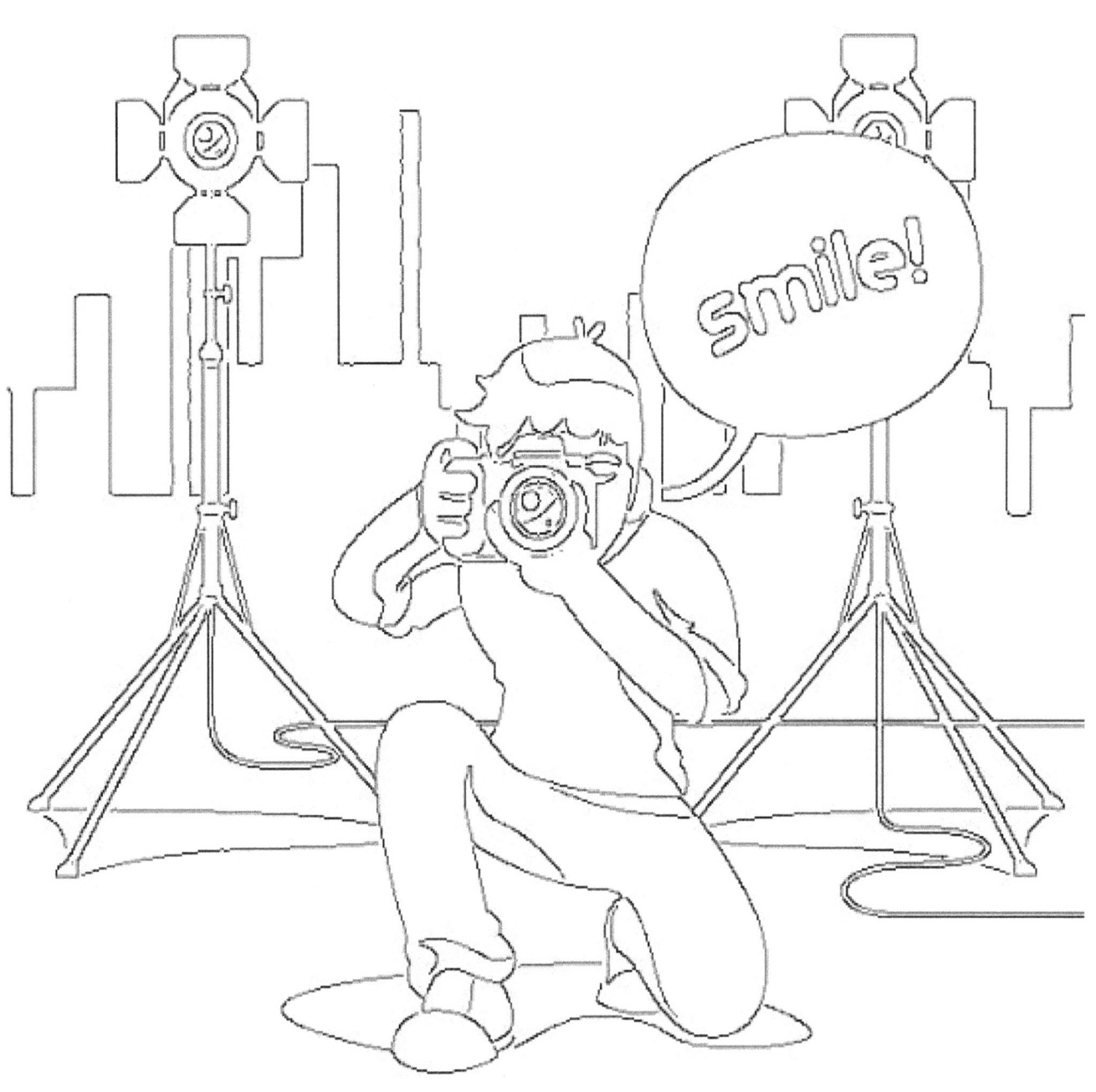

CIVIL ENGINEER

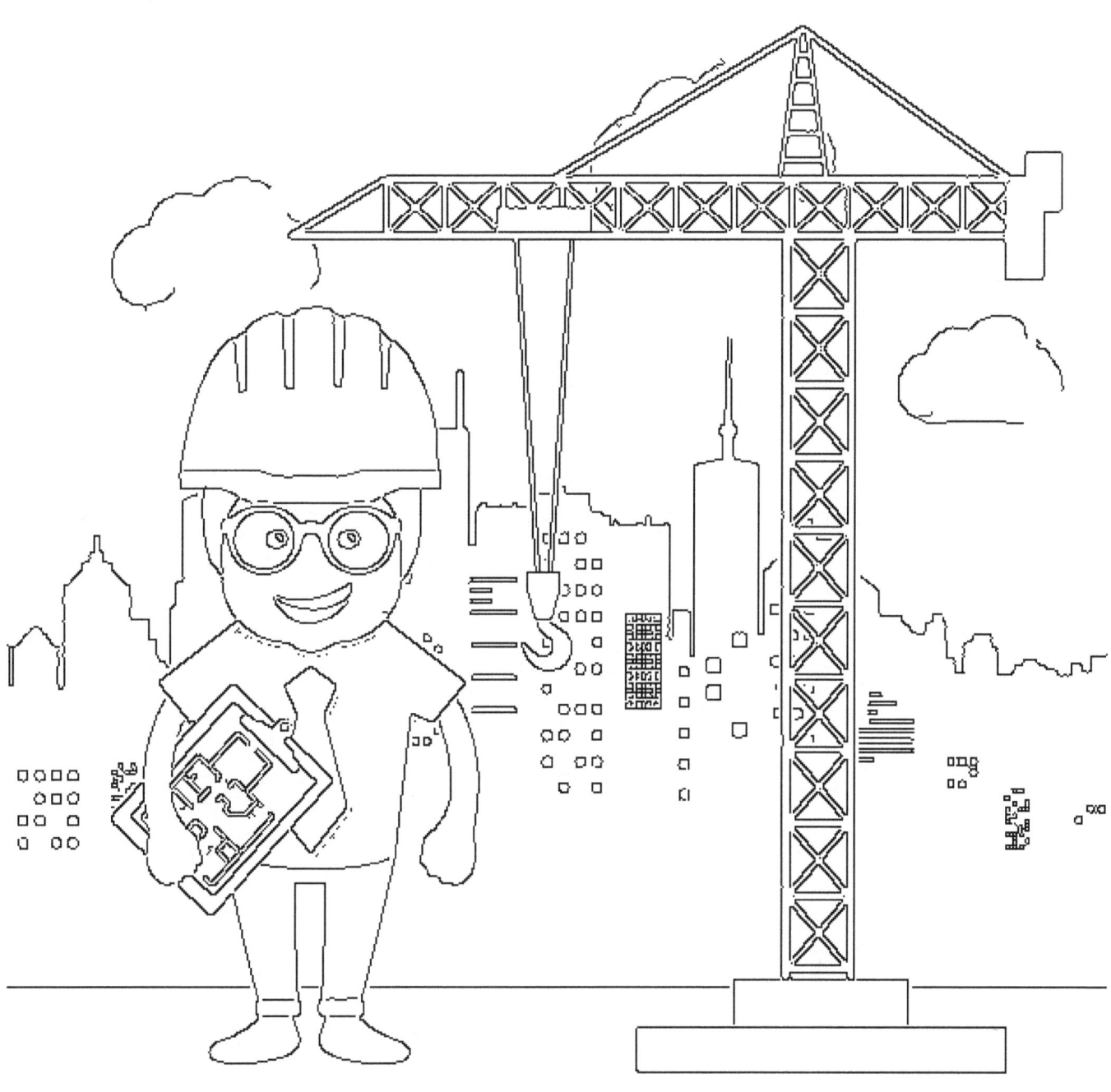

SINGER

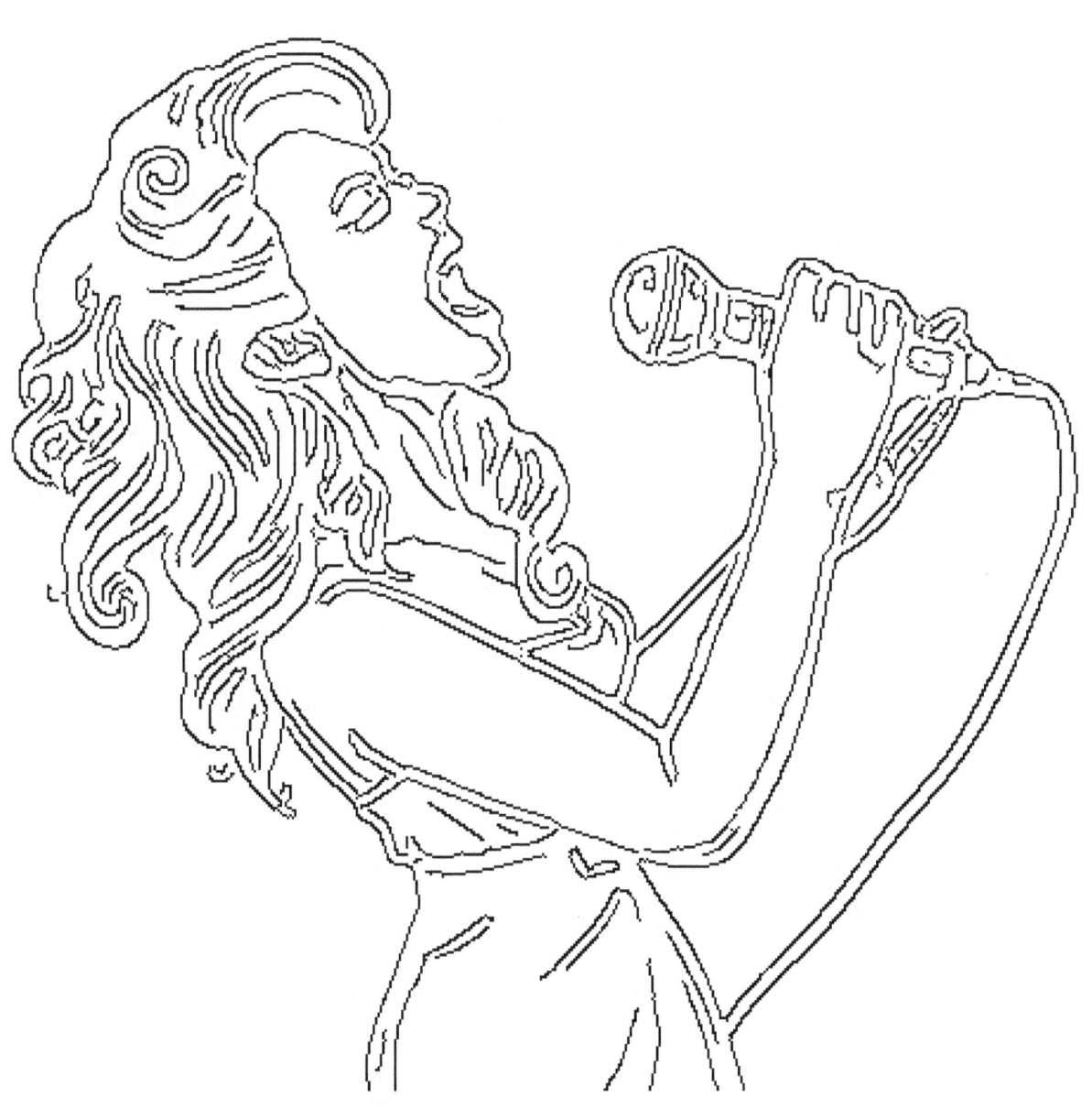

REPORTER

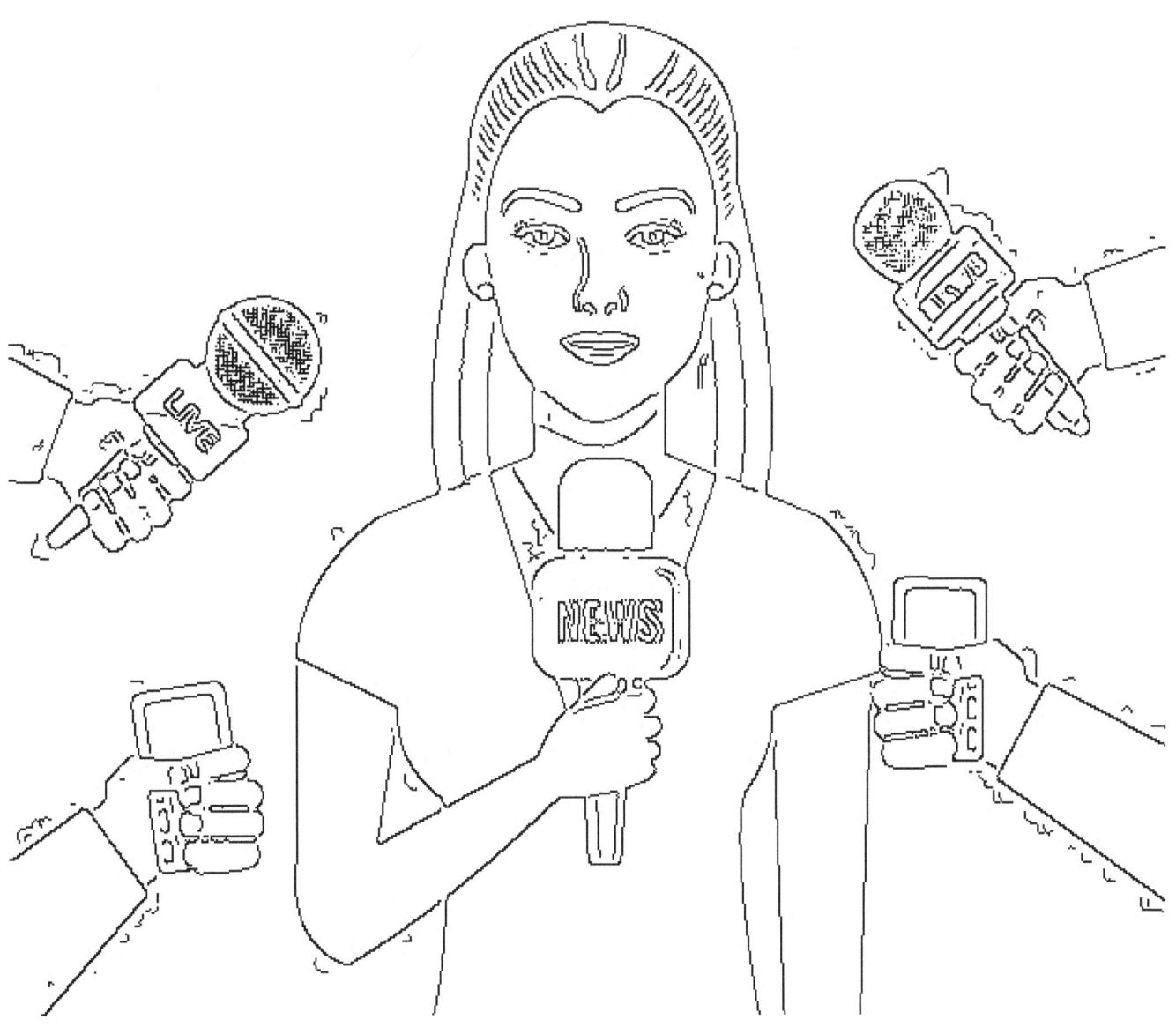

ATHLETE

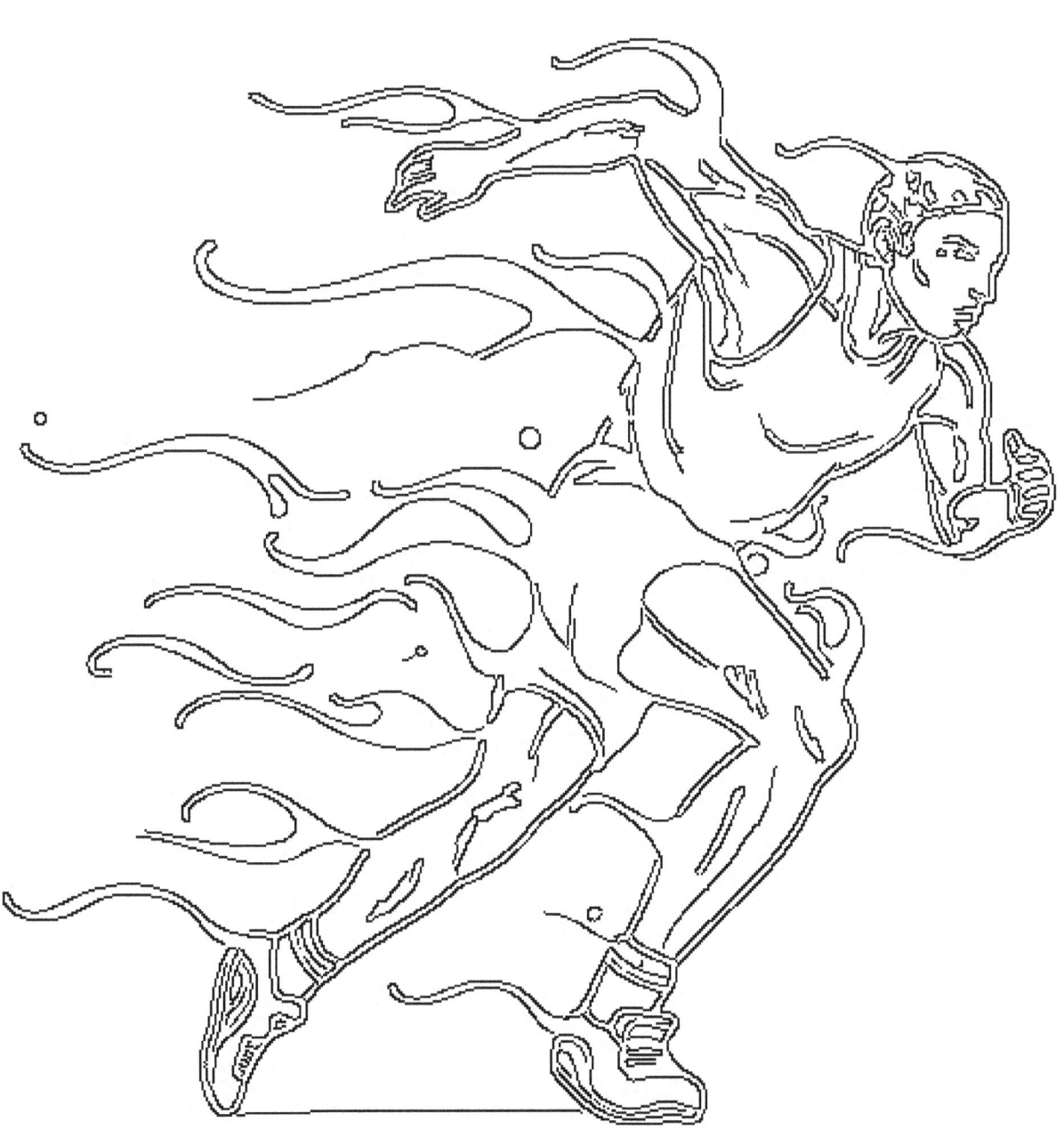

BASEBALL PLAYER

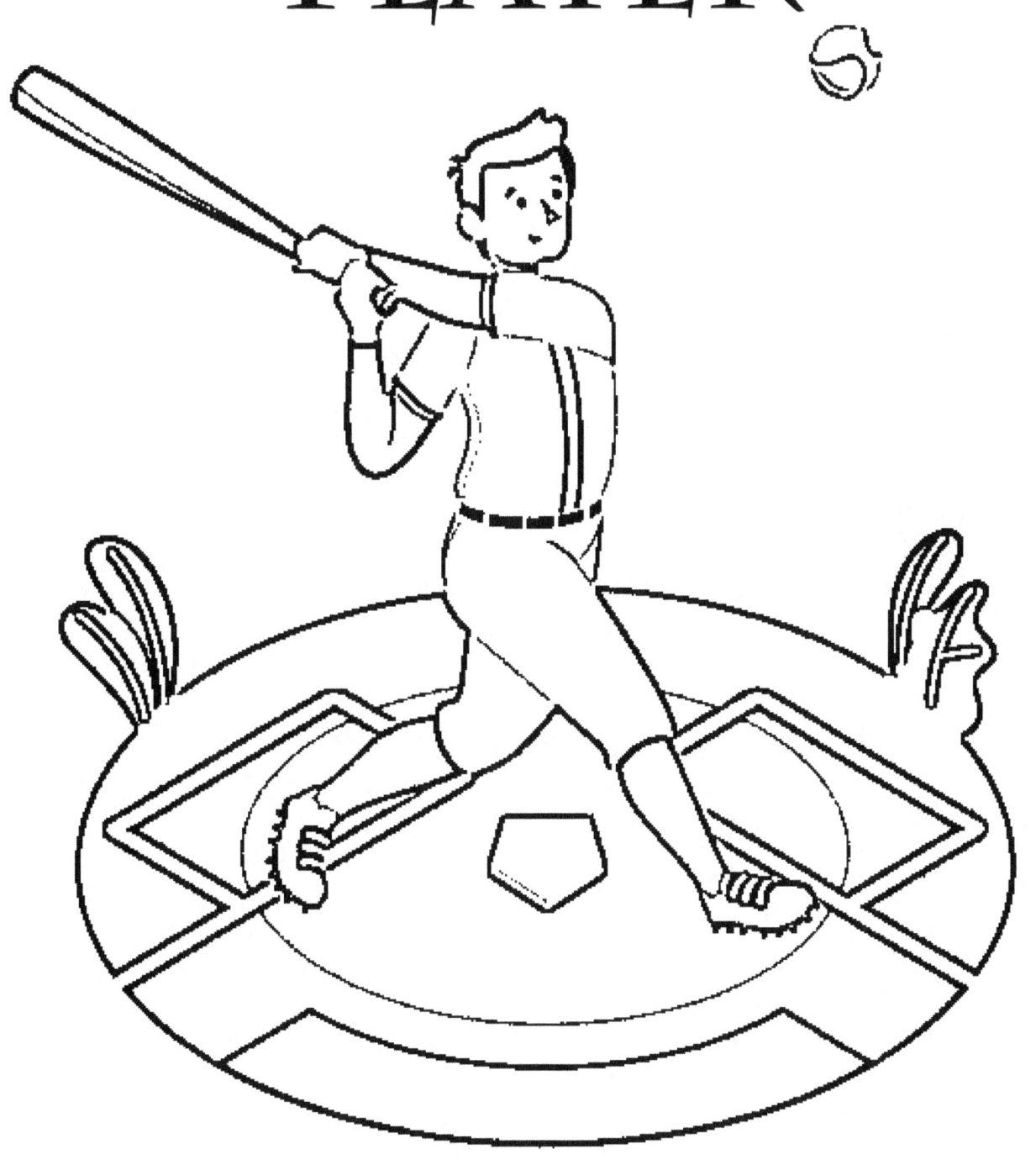

TENNIS PLAYER

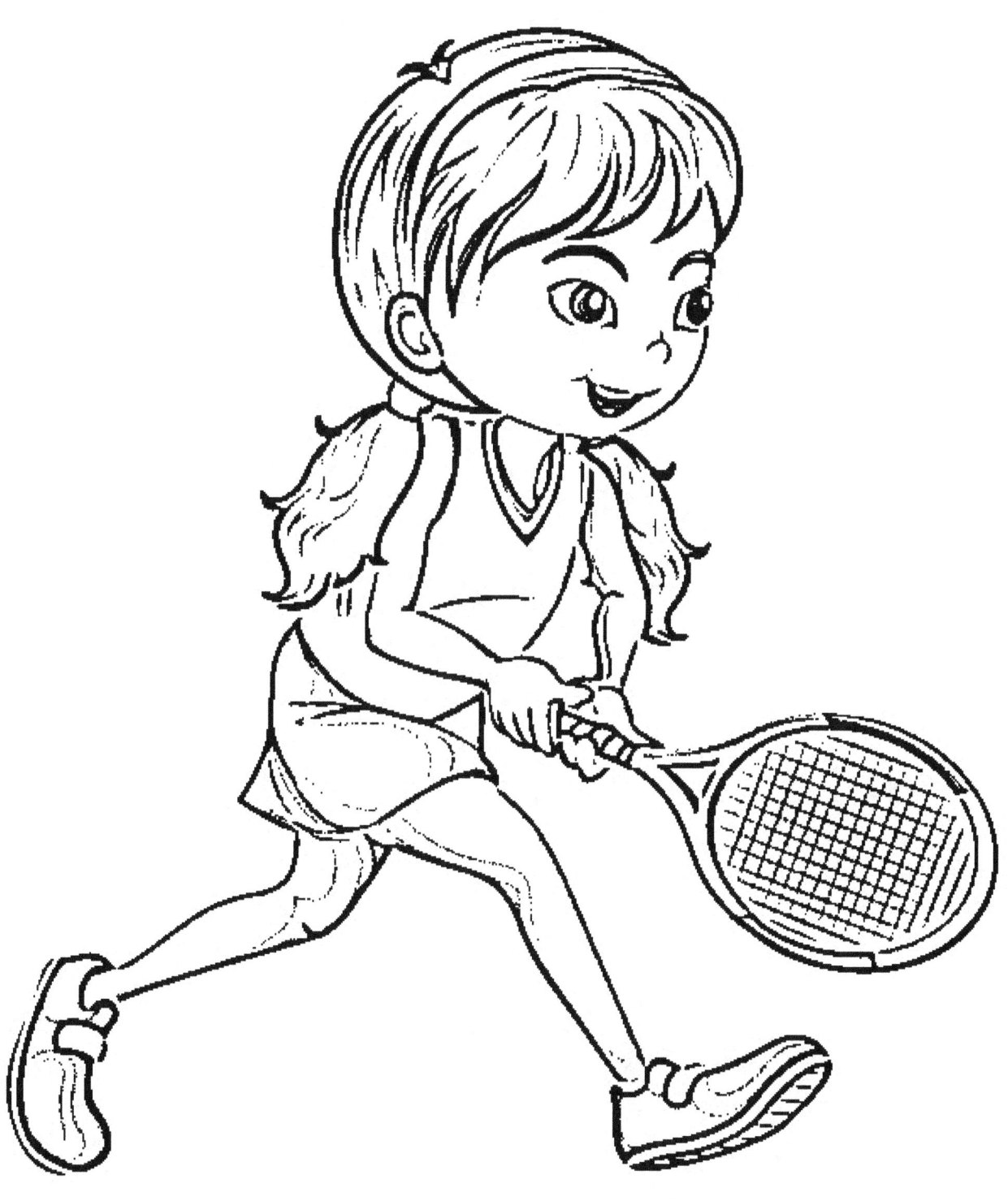

FARMER

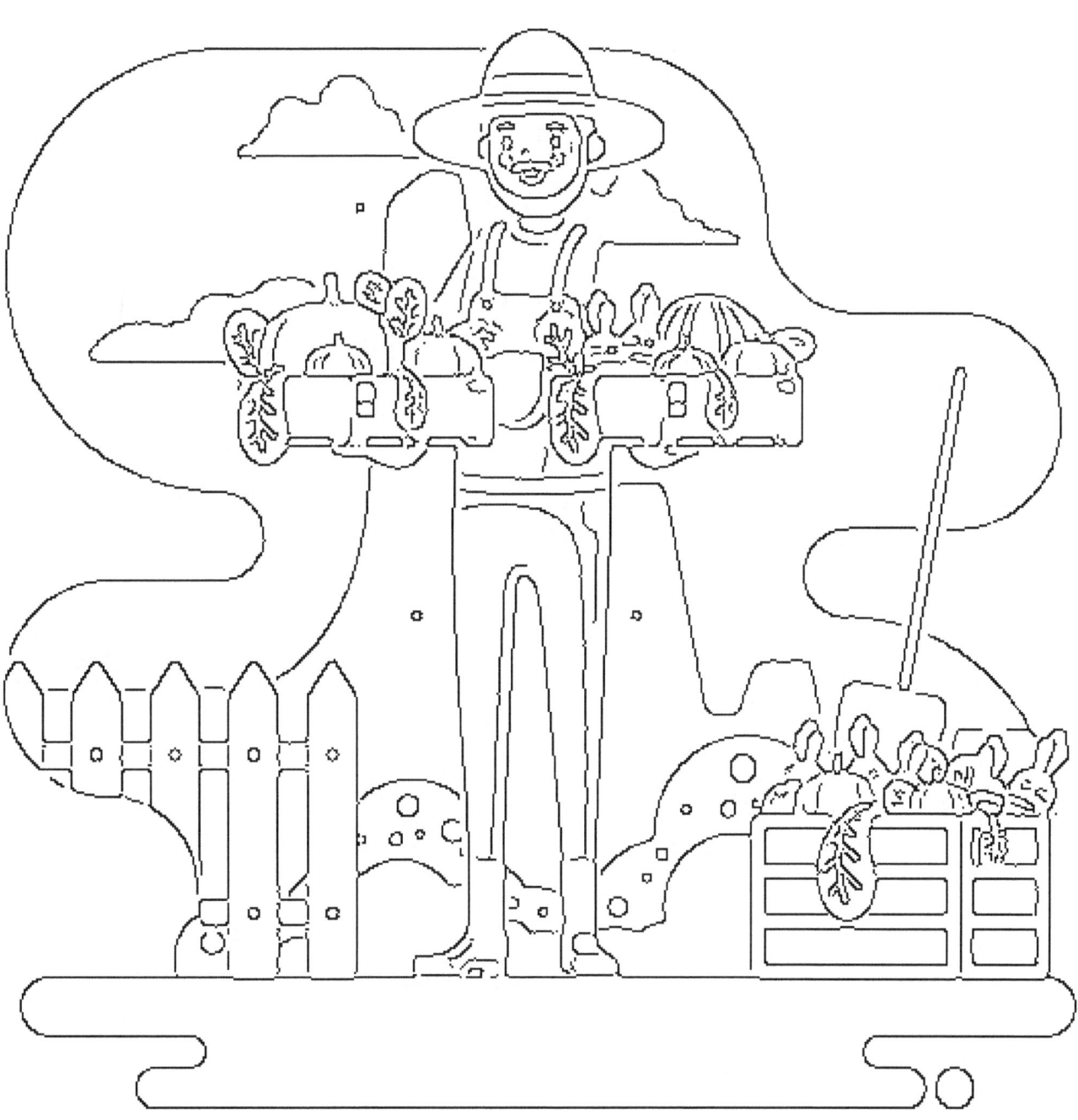

BUTCHER

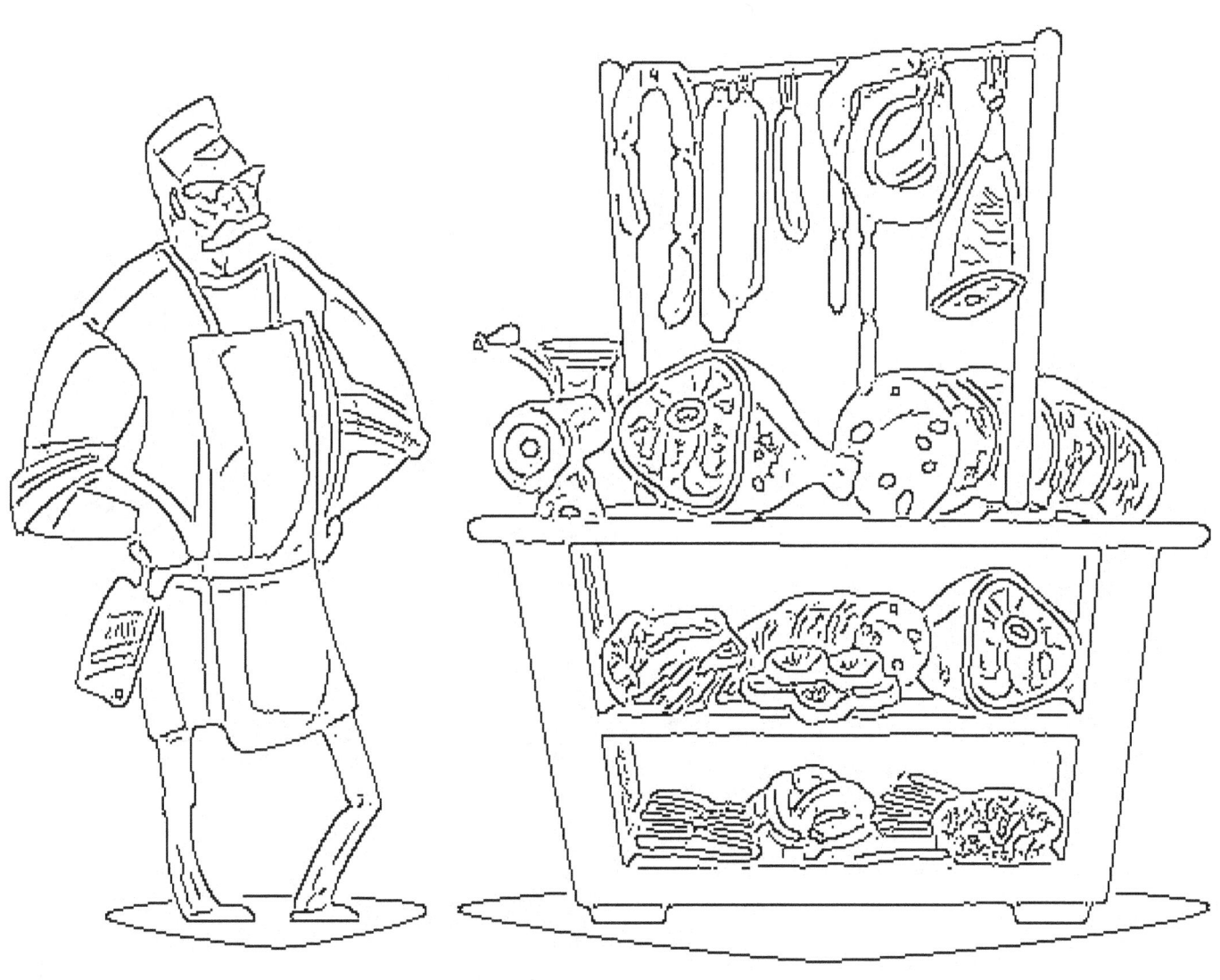

CARPENTER

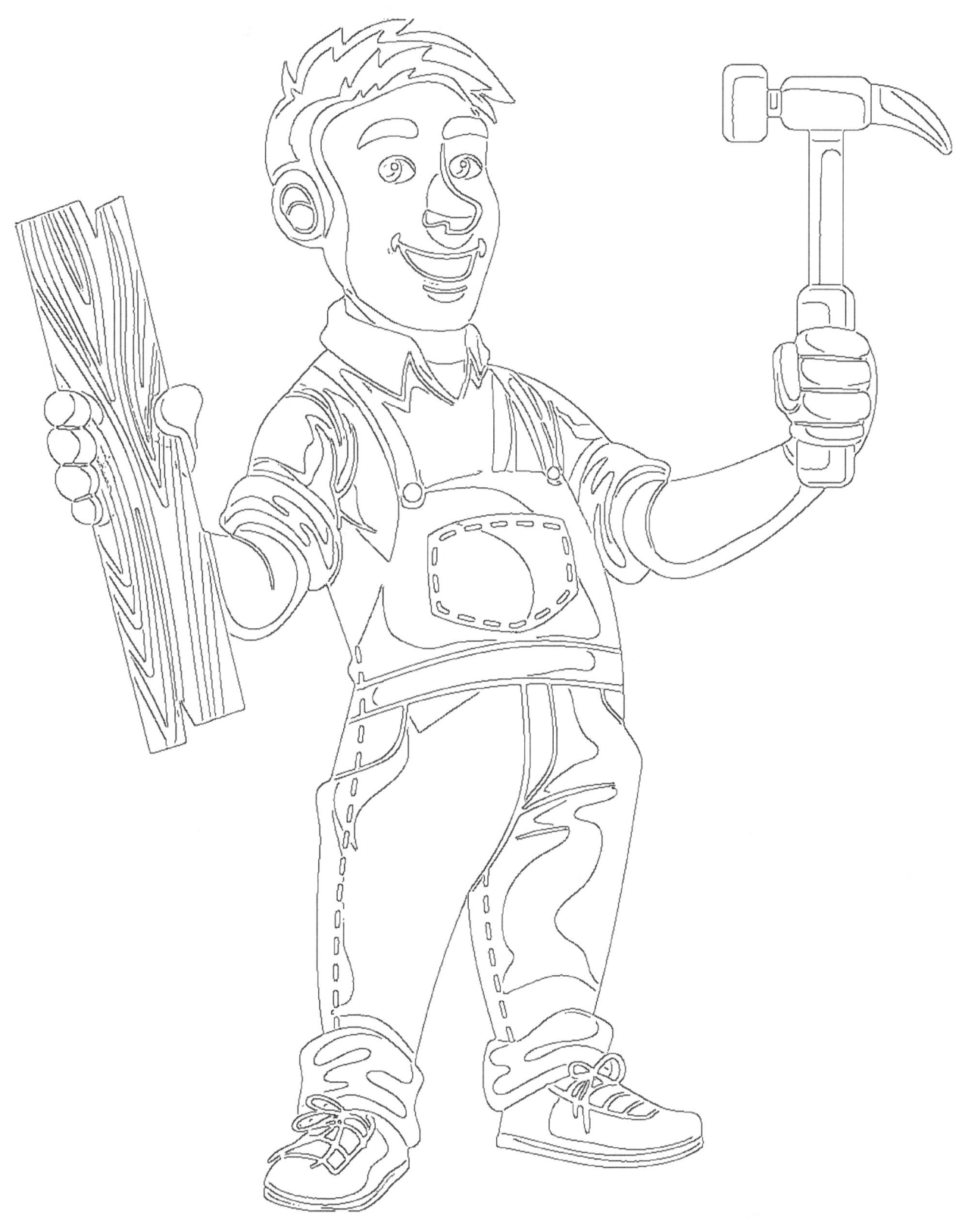

PAINTER

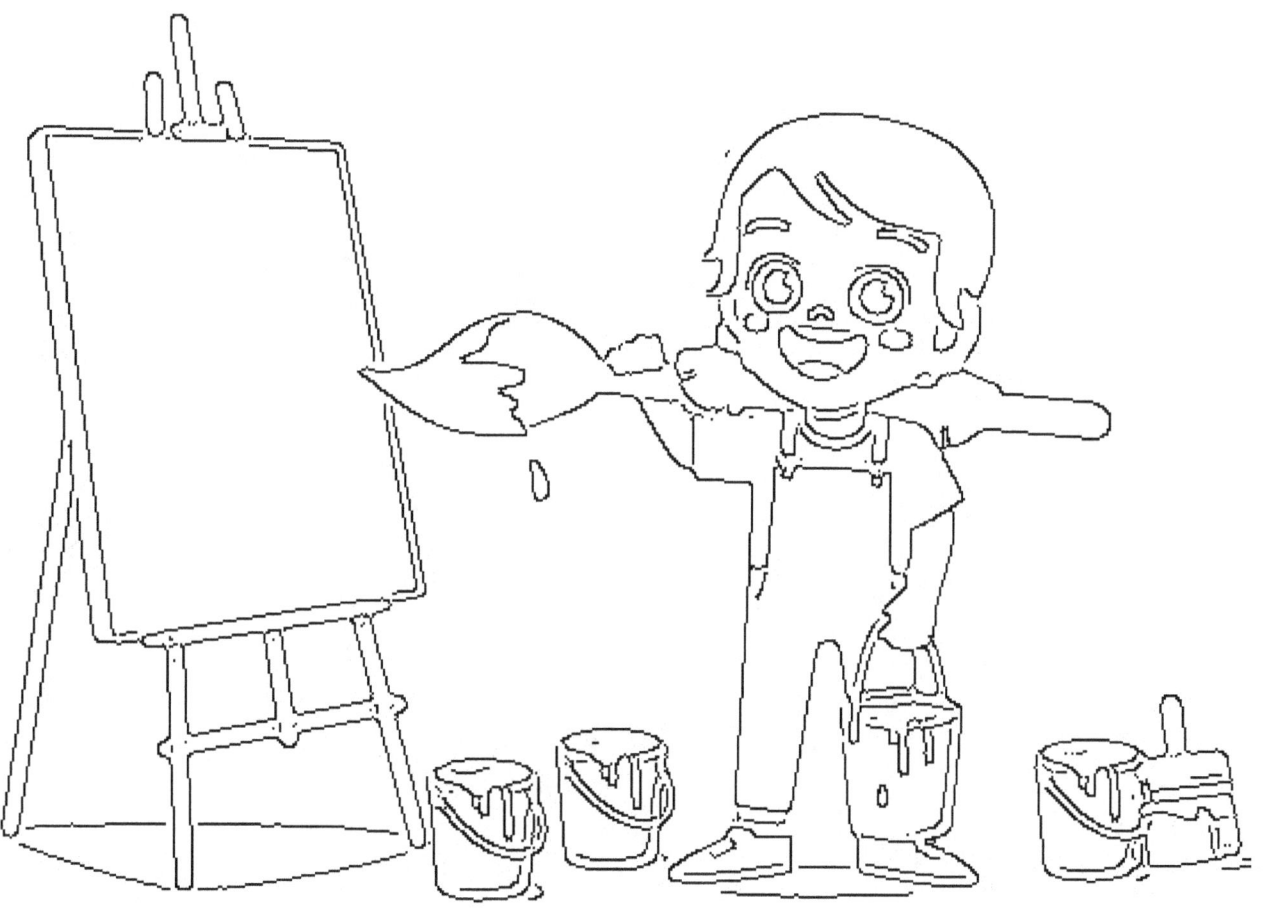

FLORIST

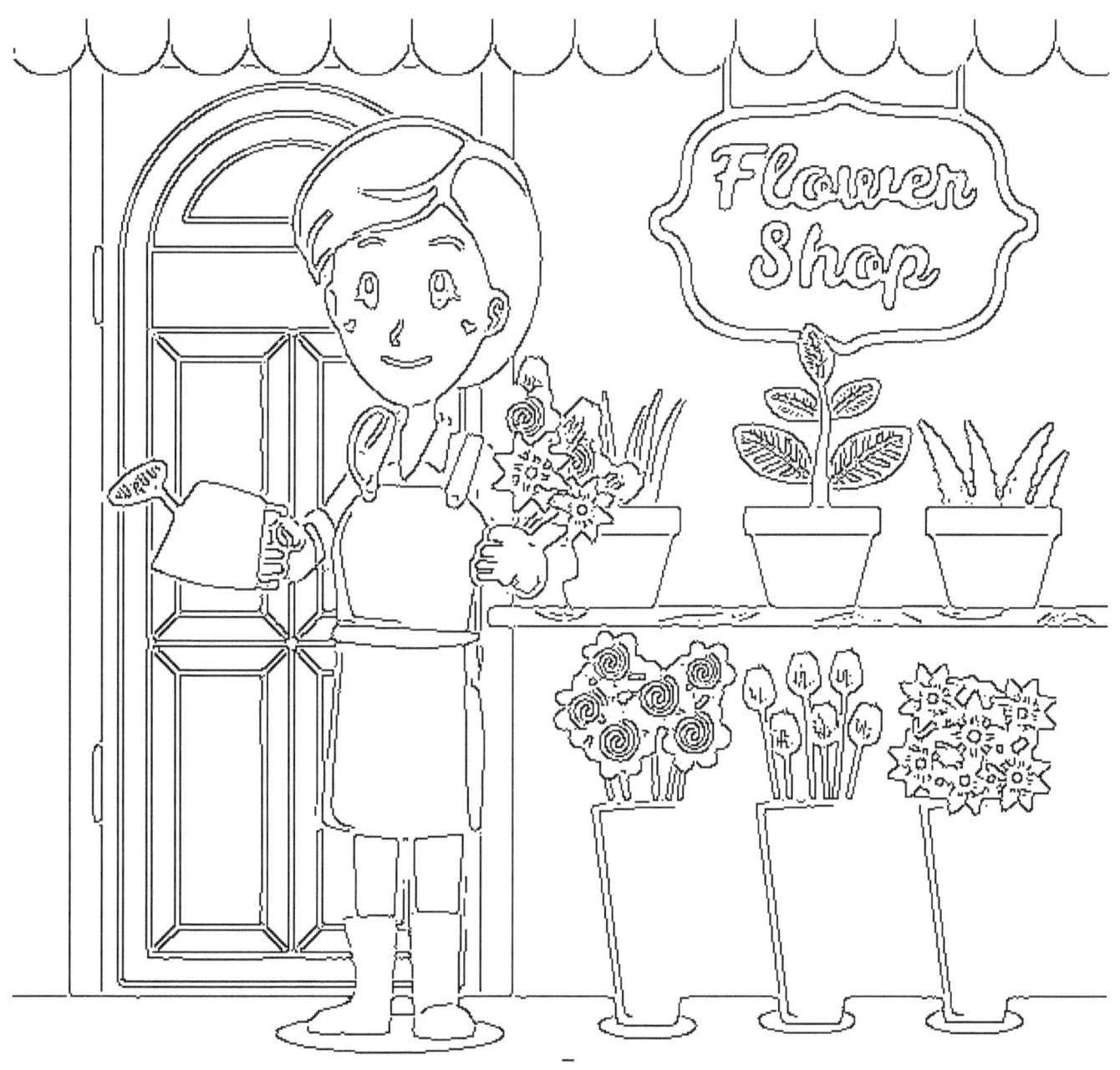

POSTMAN

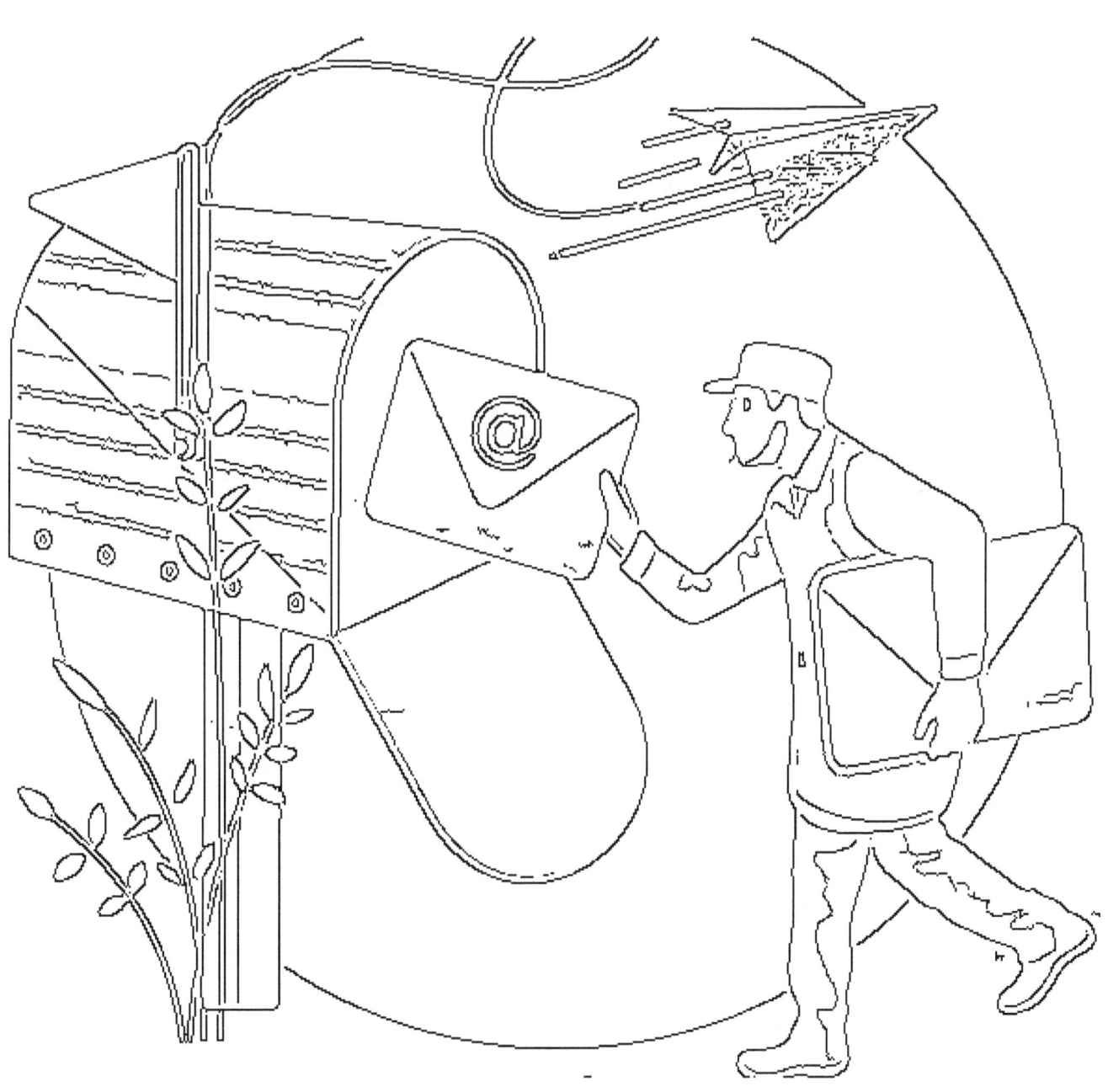

LIFEGUARD

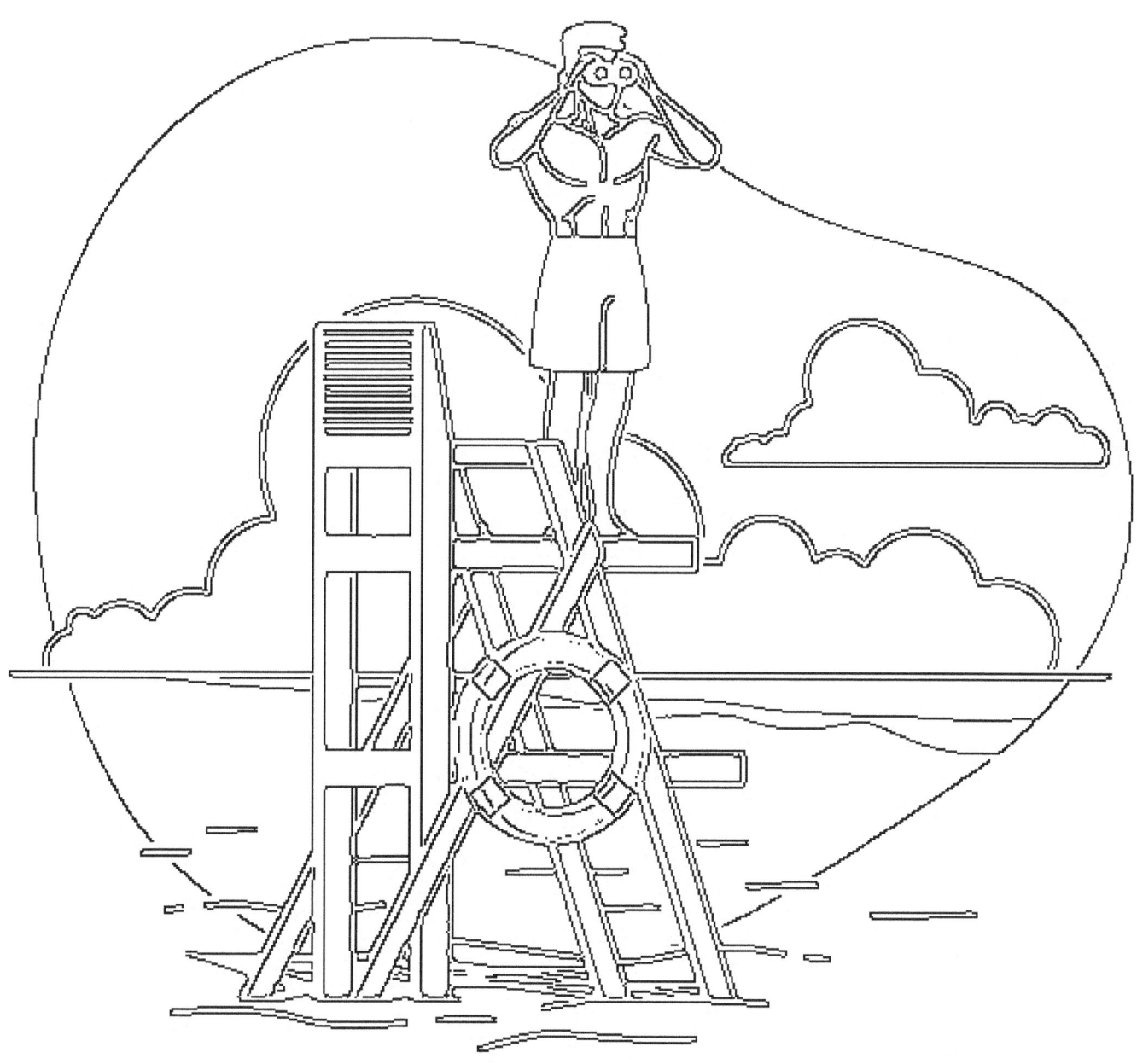